TRACING YOUR GLASGOW ANCESTORS

FAMILY HISTORY FROM PEN & SWORD

Tracing Secret Service Ancestors

Tracing Your Air Force Ancestors

Tracing Your Ancestors

Tracing Your Ancestors from 1066 to 1837

Tracing Your Ancestors Through Death Records

Tracing Your Ancestors Through Family Photographs

Tracing Your Ancestors Using the Census

Tracing Your Ancestors' Childhood

Tracing Your Ancestors' Parish Records

Tracing Your Aristocratic Ancestors

Tracing Your Army Ancestors – 2nd Edition

Tracing Your Birmingham Ancestors

Tracing Your Black Country Ancestors

Tracing Your British Indian Ancestors

Tracing Your Canal Ancestors

Tracing Your Channel Islands Ancestors

Tracing Your Coalmining Ancestors

Tracing Your Criminal Ancestors

Tracing Your East Anglian Ancestors

Tracing Your East End Ancestors

Tracing Your Edinburgh Ancestors

Tracing Your First World War Ancestors

Tracing Your Great War Ancestors: The Gallipoli Campaign

Tracing Your Great War Ancestors: The Somme

Tracing Your Great War Ancestors: Ypres

Tracing Your Huguenot Ancestors

Tracing Your Jewish Ancestors

Tracing Your Labour Movement Ancestors

Tracing Your Lancashire Ancestors

Tracing Your Leeds Ancestors

Tracing Your Legal Ancestors

Tracing Your Liverpool Ancestors

Tracing Your London Ancestors

Tracing Your Medical Ancestors

Tracing Your Merchant Navy Ancestors

Tracing Your Naval Ancestors

Tracing Your Northern Ancestors

Tracing Your Pauper Ancestors

Tracing Your Police Ancestors

Tracing Your Prisoner of War Ancestors: The First World War

Tracing Your Railway Ancestors

Tracing Your Royal Marine Ancestors

Tracing Your Rural Ancestors

Tracing Your Scottish Ancestors

Tracing Your Second World War Ancestors

Tracing Your Servant Ancestors

Tracing Your Service Women Ancestors

Tracing Your Shipbuilding Ancestors

Tracing Your Tank Ancestors

Tracing Your Textile Ancestors

Tracing Your Trade and Craftsmen Ancestors

Tracing Your Welsh Ancestors

Tracing Your West Country Ancestors

Tracing Your Yorkshire Ancestors

TRACING YOUR GLASGOW ANCESTORS

A Guide for Family and Local Historians

Ian Maxwell

Pen & Sword
FAMILY HISTORY

First published in Great Britain in 2017
PEN & SWORD FAMILY HISTORY
an imprint of
Pen & Sword Books Ltd
47 Church Street
Barnsley
South Yorkshire
S70 2AS

Copyright © Ian Maxwell, 2017

ISBN 978 1 47386 721 5

The right of Ian Maxwell to be identified as Author of the Work has been asserted by him in accordance with the Copyright, Designs and Patents Act 1988.

A CIP catalogue record for this book is available from the British Library.

All rights reserved. No part of this book may be reproduced or transmitted in any form or by any means, electronic or mechanical including photocopying, recording or by any information storage and retrieval system, without permission from the Publisher in writing.

Typeset in Palatino and Optima by CHIC GRAPHICS

Printed and bound in England by
CPI Group (UK), Croydon, CR0 4YY

Pen & Sword Books Ltd incorporates the imprints of Pen & Sword Archaeology, Atlas, Aviation, Battleground, Discovery, Family History, History, Maritime, Military, Naval, Politics, Railways, Select, Social History, Transport, True Crime, Claymore Press, Frontline Books, Leo Cooper, Praetorian Press, Remember When, Seaforth Publishing and Wharncliffe.

For a complete list of Pen & Sword titles please contact
PEN & SWORD BOOKS LTD
47 Church Street, Barnsley, South Yorkshire, S70 2AS, England
E-mail: enquiries@pen-and-sword.co.uk
Website: www.pen-and-sword.co.uk

CONTENTS

Introduction   1

Chapter 1   Researching in Glasgow   10
Chapter 2   Glasgow's History   22
Chapter 3   Key Sources   36
Chapter 4   Local Government and Taxation   48
Chapter 5   Land and Property Ownership   57
Chapter 6   The Church in Glasgow   65
Chapter 7   Trade and Industry   78
Chapter 8   Transport   94
Chapter 9   Education   108
Chapter 10   Health and Welfare   120
Chapter 11   Migration   129
Chapter 12   Glasgow at War   141
Chapter 13   Sport and Entertainment   153
Chapter 14   Law and Order   165
Chapter 15   Local Detail   181

Appendix – Scottish Websites   184
Bibliography   196
Index   198

INTRODUCTION

This book is about how you can trace your ancestors in Scotland's largest city and the fourth largest in the United Kingdom. It is designed for a wide audience: for the beginner who will refer to it frequently as they become familiar with the historical terms and technical information, and for the experienced researcher who is keen to tap into underused sources. Extensive cross-referencing allows the reader to follow many paths and to see the relationships between historical events, people and themes. Above all, it is intended as a handbook that can be taken to archives and libraries as a quick means of reference which, I trust, will enhance what is a fascinating subject.

Of course, searching for your family history is not simply a matter of looking at old records or scrolling through the bewildering array of information available online. Once you have found out where your forebears lived and are buried visit the places if you can – you may be lucky and some of the old houses and buildings mentioned in the records will have survived. Visiting such places can give you a better idea of the world your ancestor inhabited and, at the very least, offers the opportunity to visit one of Britain's most fascinating and vibrant cities.

THE CITY

Many people have an image of Glasgow as a large industrial city dominated by grimy Victorian tenements. It is therefore a surprise to find the origins of the city date back to the late sixth century and the arrival of St Kentigern (also known as St Mungo), who founded a church made of wattle and clay at a spot where Glasgow cathedral now stands. But it was not until the eighteenth century that Glasgow grew from a modest university town to become Britain's main hub of transatlantic trade with North America and the West Indies. This

Valentine's postcard of Glasgow cathedral and Necropolis, 1893.

was reflected in its fine streets and public buildings. Daniel Defoe visited the city in 1724 and thought Glasgow 'a very fine city; the four principal streets are the fairest for breath, and the finest built that I have ever seen in one city together'. It impressed him most as 'a city of business; here is the face of trade, as well foreign as home trade; and, I may say, 'tis the only city in Scotland, at this time, that apparently increases and improves in both'. 'In a word', he concluded, ''tis one of the cleanest, most beautiful, and best-built cities in Great Britain'.

By the onset of the Industrial Revolution, the population and economy of Glasgow and the surrounding region expanded rapidly to become one of the world's pre-eminent centres of chemicals, textiles and engineering, most notably in the shipbuilding and marine engineering industry. In doing so it absorbed migrants from the Scottish Lowlands, Highlands and Ireland in rapidly increasing numbers. By the end of the nineteenth century it could justifiably lay claim for itself the title of 'Second City of the British Empire'.

Introduction

The twentieth century saw the city enter a lengthy period of economic decline and rapid de-industrialisation, leading to high unemployment, urban decay and a reduced population by the 1960s. In the 1990s, however, it emerged again from its industrial past as European City of Culture in 1990, the UK City of Architecture and Design in 1999 and host of the Commonwealth Games in 2014. Today Glasgow has some of the best-financed and most imaginative museums and galleries in Britain – among them the showcase **Burrell Collection** and the palatial **Kelvingrove Art Gallery and Museum**, and a the surprising variety of architecture, from long rows of sandstone terraces to the elegant Art Nouveau designs of Charles Rennie Mackintosh.

HOW TO USE THIS BOOK

This book aims to provide a comprehensive guide to the resources available to both the family and local historian within Glasgow and surrounding area. It also offers an introduction to different facets of the city's history.

Many general sources, such as censuses, parish registers and civil registration indexes are now available online. While these are covered in detail here, the book also encourages you to go further and deeper, seeking out sources that you may not have considered previously. Only by digging down into the lives of our ancestors will you be able to understand how they lived and worked in a city that was constantly growing and changing.

Where relevant, references are given to original sources within the catalogues of the archives concerned. Many of these collections are not online and need to be consulted at the Mitchell Library, one of Europe's largest public libraries; with its distinctive green dome, the building has been one of the city's iconic landmarks since it opened in 1911.

A NOTE ABOUT SURNAMES

It is the existence of hereditary surnames that makes it possible to trace the history of even the most humble of families. However, it is important to remember that surnames have varied significantly over the centuries, and were affected by local dialect, pronunciation and inconsistency in spelling until well into the nineteenth century.

Surnames began to be used in Scotland from the twelfth century, and became common in the fourteenth. During the twelfth century some families of French or English extraction who already had hereditary surnames became major landowners in the country. These included families such as Bruce, Balliol, Fraser, Graham and Stuart. The spread of recognisable surnames in Scotland, nevertheless, appears to have been slow. As late as the fourteenth century the surnames used by the majority in the Lowlands of Scotland do not appear to have been substantially different in their general character from those employed in England at the same time.

The general spread of heritary surnames in the Lowlands was not complete until the sixteenth century. There were many cases where tenants or other dependents of major landowners assumed their overlords' surnames as their own. The surnames Graham and Stewart, both common in Glasgow, are examples of the process whereby tenants assumed the name of their masters.

It is worth examining the twenty most popular surnames in Glasgow according to the 1881 census as a means of exploring their origin and history. According to the 1881 census, the twenty most common surnames found in Glasgow were:

Smith	Reid
Campbell	Scott
Brown	Hamilton
Wilson	Walker
Thomson	Cameron
Stewart	Graham
Anderson	Ferguson
Robertson	Clark
Murray	Watson
Miller	Kelly

Introduction

Surnames from personal names with the addition of '-son' occur from the thirteenth century onwards. It is therefore not surprising to find that Glasgow has a high quota of patronymics with the Lowland names Thomson (5th most common), Ferguson (17th), Robertson (8th), Wilson (4th), Anderson (7th) and Watson (19th) all popular.

Most late-mediaeval trades are commemorated in occupational names. Smith is the commonest name in Scotland and most popular in Glasgow at the end of the nineteenth century. Miller can be as an occupational surname for a miller or a toponymic surname for people from a locale in Glasgow. Miller was also adopted by immigrants from other European countries with surnames of similar origin such as Mueller, Müller and Mühler.

The great prevalence of certain leading surnames in various towns and villages in Scotland led to the increasing use of nicknames to identify individuals: Brown (the second commonest name in Scotland and third most popular in nineteenth-century Glasgow), Black, Gray, White, Small and Young are common to both Scotland and England. One of the most celebrated of Highland names – Campbell – belongs to the nickname class (second most common name in Glasgow in 1881). In Scotland, Campbell derives from two Scottish Gaelic words, 'Cam' and 'Béal' meaning 'crooked mouth' or 'wry-mouthed'.

Another type of nickname is racial in character. Scott (twelfth most common surname in 1881) is perhaps the most famous of these names; it dates from the time when non-Scottish inhabitants of North Britain (in the form of Britons, Angles and Normans) were still clearly identifiable.

It is dangerous to make too many assumptions about the origin of an ancestor based solely on a surname. For example, the surname Murray (9th) was originally a localised Scottish name derived from the region now called Moray. However it may be of Irish origin from the anglicised form of the name Muireach, a contracted form of Muireadhach. Likewise, Reed has more than one spelling (i.e. Reid, Read and Reade), and more than one explanation. Reid, the most

View of Old Stockwell Bridge, Glasgow, 1828. (Mitchell Library, GC 941.435 GOR)

common form in Scotland, is descriptive, from the Old Scots and Old English *reid* meaning 'red' and describing someone with red hair or a ruddy complexion. Cameron (fifteenth most common in Glasgow) has several possible origins. One is from a Gaelic nickname derived from *cam* ('crooked', 'bent') and *sròn* ('nose'). Another is from any of the various places called Cameron, especially such places located in Fife. Hamilton most probably originated in the village of Hamilton, Leicestershire, England but bearers of that name became established in the thirteenth century in Lanarkshire, Scotland.

Of the top twenty names listed in 1881, Kelly would appear to be the highest placed Irish surname. The name O'Kelly, Kelly, Kelley, Kellie and the Gaelic form O'Ceallaigh is the most common surname in Ireland. However, the surname can also be derived from several place names including two locations in Scotland: Kelly, near Arbroath; and Kellie, in Fife.

Introduction

Finally, a word about the surname Glasgow, which is particularly associated with the city. This long-established surname is of early medieval Scottish origin. It is a locational name from the old burgh, now city, of Glasgow on the River Clyde, first recorded as 'Glasgu' in 1116. The first recorded spelling of the family name is shown to be that of John de Glasgu, the Bishop of St Andrews from 1258. Today it is found all over the world, particularly in the US states of California, Texas and New York.

LOCAL HISTORY
As well as providing a guide to genealogical records, this book discusses the history of Glasgow and the surrounding area. It is only possible to sketch the city's rich history in a volume such as this. If you wish to delve further into Glasgow's past, a whole variety of sources are available. Interesting older studies are available online through the Internet Archives (www.archive.org) and Project Gutenberg (www.gutenberg.org)/ and include:

- James MacLehose, *Memoirs and portraits of one hundred Glasgow men who have died during the last thirty years and in their lives did much to make the city what it now is* (1886).
- Hugh Macintosh, *The origin and history of Glasgow streets* (1902).
- John Guthrie Smith and John Oswald Mitchell, *The old country houses of the old Glasgow gentry* (1878).
- George Stewart, *Curiosities of Glasgow citizenship As exhibited chiefly in the business career of its old commercial aristocracy* (1881).
- James Hamilton Muir, *Glasgow in 1901* (1901).
- Robert Gillespie, *Glasgow and the Clyde* (1876).
- Robert Renwick, *History of Glasgow* (1921).
- Hugh MacDonald, *Rambles Around Glasgow* (1901).

More modern histories are available at local libararies or from major booksellers. Those particularly useful are:

Tracing Your Glasgow Ancestors

- Hugh Cochrane, *Glasgow: The first 800 Years* (1975).
- J. Cowan, *From Glasgow's Treasure Chest* (1951).
- David Daiches, *Glasgow* (1982).
- Joe Fisher, *The Glasgow Encyclopaedia* (1994).
- Andrew Gibb, *Glasgow: The Making of a City* (1983).
- John Hume, *Industrial Archaeology of Glasgow* (1974).
- Irene Maver, *Glasgow* (2000).
- Charles Oakley, *The Second City* (1975).

Most districts and suburbs have their own local history society and website addresses are given in the Appendix in this volume. The **Glasgow & West of Scotland Family History Society** provides a service to assist others interested in researching their family history, http://www.gwsfhs.org.uk/.

The **Glasgow Collection** at the **Mitchell Library** is the first point of contact for anyone interested in finding material relating to the history and development of the city. Apart from books, journals and photographs, the map collection records how streets and neighbourhoods have changed over the years and local newspapers provide a fascinating insight into local events and personalities from the past. The **Virtual Mitchell** is a set of online views showing Glasgow streets and buildings as well as people going about their daily lives and can be viewed at http://www.mitchelllibrary.org/virtualmitchell/.

Charles Rennie Mackintosh (1868–1928), Scottish architect and designer.

GLASGOW ACCENT

The city of Glasgow has a very distinctive dialect and accent which is familiar to millions around the world thanks to shows like *Rab C.*

Introduction

Nesbitt and *Taggart*. At a time when many accents are slowly eroding across the country, the Glasgow accent remains robust. It has much in common with Lowland Scots but has been influenced by the speech of the Highlanders and Irish workers who migrated in large numbers to the city in the nineteenth and twentieth centuries.

It will not be a surprise to those who love the honeyed tones of actors like Bill Paterson, Peter Capaldi or James McAvoy that the Glasgow accent has many admirers. It was recently voted the sexiest accent in Britain, winning 23 per cent of the vote in a survey by British Airways of 1,000 Americans. This was confirmed through a survey by Northumbria University which asked Japanese people to listen to the accents of six English speakers and rate them on a range of personality traits. The Glasgow accent came out on top for social attractiveness.

For those who want to explore its richness, HarperCollins publishes a Scots dictionary entitled *Collins Pocket Scots Dictionary* which lists many Glasgow Scots words and expressions spoken in the Glaswegian vernacular.

Chapter 1

RESEARCHING IN GLASGOW

SCOPE
So what do we mean by Glasgow? This may seem a strange question to ask of a city of nearly 600,000. But for the family historian the answer is not quite so straightforward. Indeed, it may be a surprise to learn that the extent of Glasgow's boundaries has caused a great deal of heated debate over the centuries between the independent burghs and villages outside the city boundaries and the expansionist plans of Glasgow Town Council and later Glasgow Corporation.

Many of the areas that we commonly consider to be an integral part of Glasgow were only absorbed in the city boundaries during the later nineteenth and early twentieth centuries. The first major change of the nineteenth century took place in 1845 when Calton, Anderston, Maryhill, Hillhead, Crosshill, East and West Pollokshields, Govanhill and a few smaller areas were annexed and more than doubled the territory of the old burgh. Up to that point the burghs of Anderston and Calton, along with most of Gorbals, had enjoyed a separate history.

Anderston was established as a new weaving village by James Anderston, the owner of nearby Stobcross in the 1720s. By the 1730s it had become an important centre of calico printing and within a hundred years had grown so large that it was essentially part of Glasgow when it was formally annexed. The old village of **Calton** had been a burgh in its own right since 1817. Once a village of domestic weavers, it was absorbed into the industries of the Clyde and attracted large number of Irish workers seeking employment in the new industrial economy.

Researching in Glasgow

Gorbals, a village in the parish of Govan until 1771, had served as an isolation colony for lepers from medieval times. By the 1730s a colony of weavers and brewers was established in the area and by the nineteenth century it was a major centre of the shipbuilding industry. With the addition of Gorbals, the city for the first time included land on the south side of the Clyde.

Within a decade after 1846, new efforts were being made to absorb the growing villages outside the city's boundaries. The town council acquired the West End's **Kelvingrove Park** in 1852 and the substantial south-side lands of Pathhead for development as **Queen's Park**. In 1872 there was a minor boundary extension which added most of Springburn, a centre for locomotive building situated in the north-east. Also annexed was **Alexandra Park**, next to the residential suburb of Dennistoun, where a new municipal park provided much-needed leisure facilities for the heavily populated East End of the city.

By the 1880s, with over half a million Glasgow inhabitants and only marginal boundary increases since 1846, the town council once again made a bid to extend its jurisdiction. Their high-profile campaign resulted in the setting up of the parliamentary boundary commission of 1888, which three years later doubled the city's territory to just over 18 square miles. All the police burghs were included (Govanhill, Crosshill, Pollokshields, Hillhead and Maryhill), with the exception of Govan, Kinning Park and Partick. Glasgow also absorbed the northern districts of Balornock, Possilpark, Ruchill and part of Springburn, the south-side territories of Bellahouston, Crossmyloof, Langside, Mount Florida, Polmadie, Shawlands and Strathbungo, and Kelvinside in the west.

Glasgow continued to expand during the late nighteenth century absorbing areas such as Craigton (1896) and Blackhill, Provanmill and Riddrie (1899) and Kinning Park (1905). The next substantial increase came in the 1912 extension which took the number of Glasgow's inhabitants to over a million and extended the city boundaries to nearly 30 square miles. This expansion included the historic burgh of **Pollokshaws**, as well as the southern districts of

St Enoch Square. (Postcard published by Raphael Tuck & Sons Ltd, 1949)

Newlands and Cathcart. Among areas added in the west were Anniesland, Dawsholm, Jordanhill and Scotstoun, while the acquisition of Shettleston and Tollcross represented Glasgow's first major movement eastwards since 1846.

Govan and **Partick** were also incorporated into the city, against much local opposition. Govan village, on the south bank of the Clyde, was of great antiquity, the old parish church supposedly occupying the site of a Celtic foundation. Although Partick remained a village until the middle of the eighteenth century, it is an ancient place. The Kings of Strathclyde had a residence there, and in 1136 David I (1124–53) granted the lands of Perdyc to the see of Glasgow. During the nineteenth century it was transformed from a weaving village of 1,000 to a major shipbuilding centre, with a population of 56,000 by the time of its annexation.

Until the Second World War Glasgow's population continued to increase, reaching a peak of 1,128,473 in 1939, making it one of the most densely populated cities in the world. The council's policy from the 1950s of building high-rise housing was one factor in the

Researching in Glasgow

destruction of a group of long-established communities which made up much of working class Glasgow until the 1960s. Maryhill, Partick, Govan, Gorbals and Ibrox were places where, in some cases until the 1970s, several generations of the same family had grown up and continued to live in these self-contained and self-sufficient communities. Many of those rehoused found homes in the new towns of East Kilbride, Cumbernauld and Erskine. Many others moved to the sprawling peripheral housing schemes of Easterhouse, Castlemilk and Drumchapel.

The creation of Strathclyde Regional Council in May 1975 covered the whole of the former counties of Ayrshire, Bute, Dunbartonshire, Lanarkshire and Renfrewshire, almost all of Argyllshire, part of Stirlingshire and the whole of Glasgow City. Strathclyde Regional Council inherited the powers and duties of the former county councils and Glasgow Corporation, including responsibility for schools and police. However, plans to create a 'Greater Glasgow' were largely unsuccessful and areas like Cambsland and Rutherglen which were added at this time were removed in 1996 when the Conservative government dismantled Strathclyde Region. For the first time the city's territory contracted to cover less than 68.5 square miles, while reorganisation had the effect of reducing the population by 50,000.

These boundary changes, together with the comprehensive urban renewal projects in the 1960s which resulted in large-scale relocation of people to new towns and peripheral suburbs, reduced the population of the City of Glasgow council area to 578,000 inhabitants in 2001 – half the number of Glaswegians in 1938.

So you can see just how difficult it can be to fix boundaries to the area you are researching. You need to be constantly aware of where you are researching and which jurisdictions apply, and at which period. For the purposes of this book, Glasgow is defined as being all of the area now covered by the City of Glasgow within its 1975 boundaries which includes the former county of the city of Glasgow and a number of areas previously within the county of Lanark: Cambuslang (Central and North, and South lying outwith East

Kilbride), Rutherglen (including the burgh of Rutherglen), part of Carmunnock area (that lying outwith East Kilbride) and Baillieston, Carmyle, Garrowhill, Mount Vernon and Springboig.

PRINCIPAL ARCHIVES
The Glasgow area is served by a diverse range of archives of major national importance. Before you visit check each organisation's website for details of opening times and cost of services as well as up-to-date information on collections and online resources.

Mitchell Library
Mitchell Library
North Street, Glasgow G3 7DN
0141 287 2999
libraries@glasgowlife.org.uk

Since its opening in 1877 the Mitchell Library has made a speciality of collecting local material – books, illustrations, maps, photographs and newspapers relating to Glasgow. It has also specialised in Scottish topography and history, particularly clan and family history. The **City Archives** are also housed in the Mitchell Library. In addition to the records of the former Glasgow Corporation, they contain those of the county councils and parish authorities within the former Strathclyde Region except for Argyllshire and Ayrshire. The records of various families and estates in the Glasgow area and a large number of businesses, including firms of solicitors, are also held. Records of particular interest to genealogists include: the records of the Glasgow incorporations of trades, including membership lists; Poor Law records, including detailed applications for poor relief to the parishes of Glasgow (from 1851), Barony (from 1861), Govan (from 1876) and a number of other parishes from various dates until 1948; the burgess rolls for Glasgow (printed to 1846, but continuing in manuscript thereafter, with indexes); records of hundreds of schools, often including admission registers, in a few cases dating from the 1860s; estate records with information about tenants; registers of some local government employees, notably the police; business records, in some cases including information about employees; and kirk session records for churches in Glasgow presbytery.

NHS Greater Glasgow and Clyde Archives
NHS Greater Glasgow and Clyde Archivist, Archive Services, University of Glasgow, 77–87 Dumbarton Road, Glasgow G11 6PW
http://www.gla.ac.uk/services/archives/

The holdings of the **NHS Greater Glasgow and Clyde Archives**, one of the largest health authority archives in the United Kingdom, consist principally of the archives of the hospitals in the Glasgow area and in Paisley. These date back to the late eighteenth century when Glasgow Royal Infirmary was established. The archive also holds the prime records of the defunct Western Regional Health Board and of the Greater Glasgow Health Board.

The archives include the minutes of governing bodies, architects' drawings of hospital buildings, photographs, accounts, correspondence, reports and records of patient care.

Glasgow University Archives
Archive Services, 13 Thurso Street, Glasgow G11 6PE
http://www.gla.ac.uk/services/archives/

The official records of the university created and accumulated since its foundation in 1451. Including university related records deposited by staff, alumni and associated organisations and the records of predecessor institutions.

The oldest records in the archive are charters dating from the thirteenth century conveying land and privileges that eventually came to the university. Special collections include the **Scottish Theatre Archive**, which is a continually expanding collection that plays an important national role in helping to preserve Scotland's theatrical heritage. The Scottish Business Archive holds records covering Scotland from the eighteenth century.

The Scottish Jewish Archives Centre
129 Hill Street, Garnethill, Glasgow G3 6UB
+44 (0)141 332 4911
info@sjac.org.uk
http://www.sjac.org.uk/

Founded in 1987 and based in Garnethill Synagogue (Scotland's oldest) in Glasgow, the Scottish Jewish Archives Centre aims to document and illustrate the religious, organisational, social, economic, political, cultural and family life of Jews in Scotland since the eighteenth century. It holds old synagogue minute books and registers, membership lists, over 6,000 photographs, oral history recordings, annual reports of many communal organisations and a small library of books of Scottish Jewish interest, friendly society regalia, personal papers, war medals, ceremonial keys, newspapers, magazines, trophies, plaques, paintings and sculptures.

Library and Archive, Royal College of Physicians & Surgeons of Glasgow
232–42 St Vincent Street, Glasgow G2 5RJ
+44 (0)141 221 6072
info@rcpsg.ac.uk, for all enquiries
https://www.rcpsg.ac.uk/

The college archive collections include a wide range of materials relating to medicine, surgery and dentistry in Glasgow and the west of Scotland. The archives of the college itself date from the early seventeenth century, with the majority of materials dating from the nineteenth and twentieth centuries. They also hold deposited archive collections from former (and present) members and fellows, and collections relating to local medical societies. The College Library and Archive services can also be used to help family history researchers trace medical, surgical or dental ancestors.

Researching in Glasgow

University of Strathclyde Archives & Special Collections
16 Richmond Street, Glasgow G1 1XQ
+44 (0)141 552 4400
https://www.strath.ac.uk/

The Archives hold the official records of the University of Strathclyde from 1796 to the present day. These include the records of the university's predecessor institutions as well as the papers of many former staff and students and associated organisations. The university archives are an outstanding resource for the study of education, science and society in Scotland.

Glasgow Caledonian University Archives & Special Collections
Glasgow Caledonian University, Cowcaddens Road, Glasgow G4 0BA
+44 (0)141 331 3000
+44 (0)141 331 3005 (fax)
http://www.gcu.ac.uk/caledoniancommunityarchives/

The Glasgow Caledonian University collections are a unique learning, teaching and research resource open to everyone. The subject strengths are the Scottish Labour and Trades Union Movement, Scottish social work, social policy and child welfare, and Scottish social enterprise. It also houses the the records of the university and its parent bodies (dating back to 1875 and the formation of the Glasgow School of Cookery).

Royal Conservatoire of Scotland Archives & Collections
100 Renfrew Street, Glasgow G2 3DB
+44 (0)141 332 4101

The RCS was originally founded as the Glasgow Athenaeum in 1847, teaching a variety of subjects, including art classes, to students in Glasgow. Their holdings include minute books, prospectuses, student records and photographs which reveal the organisation's history.

GRAVEYARDS

A walk around a graveyard can often save wading through endless pages of a church register for the birth or death dates of a particular ancestor. If you are lucky, gravestones may provide valuable information about the deceased's occupation or place of origin and might even include the names of husbands, wives or children. They may reveal the married names of daughters or sisters of your ancestors and perhaps record two, three or more generations of a family.

However, you should treat the information on a headstone (especially ages) with some care. A memorial may refer to two or more people and have been placed there on the death of the last person, perhaps many years after the death of the first person buried in the plot.

A death certificate does not indicate the place or date of burial, but your relatives may hold memorial or funeral cards. Because so many headstones can be illegible it is worth checking at your local library to find out if the gravestones in a particular cemetery have been transcribed and published.

For many years the only burying ground in Glasgow was the historic one which lay on the south side of the cathedral sloping down to the Molendinar Burn. Today it consists largely of flat, almost totally illegible tombstones. In 1719 a new burying ground was opened up on the north side of Back Cow Loan (now Ingram Street) and a new church added to it the following year. At first it was called the North West Church, but later became known as St David's (Ramshorn). The ground, initially reserved for Glasgow merchants, remained Glasgow's most fashionable burying ground throughout the latter half of the eighteenth century and into the nineteenth.

Other than pre-Reformation burials around the cathedral, there were no early Roman Catholic burying grounds in Glasgow. The first post-Reformation one recorded was St Mary's, established in Abercrombie Street in 1839; it was demolished some time in the 1960s. The two other Roman Catholic burying grounds are St Peter's Dalbeth, London Road (1851), still the responsibility of the Church, and St Kentigern's Maryhill (1882), under the control of the district council.

Researching in Glasgow

Two early Episcopal city churches had burying grounds associated with them, St Andrew-by-the-Green, Greendyke Street (1750) and Christ Church, Brook Street (1837), but both have long since disappeared. The Quakers had two burying grounds, one in Partick, for the Keith Street congregation, which was opened in 1711 and had its last burial in 1857, and another serving Stirling Square congregation in Albion Street from the 1730s to about 1800.

For much of its history the parish church held responsibility for burying the dead but there was a growing need for an alternative solution. **Glasgow Necropolis**, modelled on Père-Lachaise cemetery in Paris, officially opened in April 1833. It accepted Protestants, Catholics, Lutherans, Quakers, Jews and others. Glasgow's businessmen and academics built opulent tombs but the majority of the 50,000 buried here made do with simple memorials or nothing. The Necropolis became less fashionable in the 1960s by which time it had been taken over by Glasgow District Council.

The Necropolis was the first of a number of large burial grounds in Glasgow. To the north-east of the city **Sighthill** burial ground was opened in 1840 in Springburn which was largely occupied by the city's middle class. South of the Clyde, the **Southern Necropolis**, which opened in a series of stages between 1840 and 1850, was the first attempt to provide working class people with the opportunity of a dignified burial instead of a mass or common grave. The growing population of the East End of the city was catered for by the **Eastern Necropolis** (sometimes called Janefield), which opened in 1847.

Over forty burying grounds can be traced within the boundaries of present-day Glasgow. Over the years most of these grounds were taken over the Glasgow District Council's Parks and Recreation Department, Cemeteries and Crematoria. For more details see J. Willing and J.S. Fairie,*Burial Grounds in Glasgow: a brief guide for the genealogist* (Glasgow and West of Scotland Family History Society, 1986, repr. 1993) and visit the website, http://www.discoverglasgow.org/cemeteries/4567950319.

Glasgow City Archives holds the records of those cemeteries and crematoria run by Glasgow City Council up to 1995, as well as records for other cemeteries that have never been under local authority control. The records mainly consist of burial, lair and crematoria registers.

Burial registers are arranged by the date of burial so you need to know when a person died in order to start looking through them. If you do not know the date of death, you should obtain a copy of the death certificate. The registers vary in the amount of detail but will always include the name of the deceased and the lair number (burial plot).

Lair registers will generally give the name and address of the lair owner as well as details of all the interments. Once you have obtained a lair number, you can use the lair registers to find out who else is buried in the lair.

Cremation became increasignly popular in the twentieth century. **Cremation registers** are arranged by the date of cremation and will show if the ashes have been dispersed or interred in the crematoria grounds, or if they were returned to the family.

For earlier records the **Old Parish Registers** (for pre-1855 burials) and church records can give details of those interred in churchyards, although these records do not always survive. The Old Parish Registers are among the many resources available as part of the **ScotlandsPeople** network.

If you are unsure where to start looking, you may find clues in newspapers' death notices and obituaries or you may find a monumental inscription, which are often indexed, in **Special Collections** at the **Mitchell Library**.

Deceasedonline.com
Deceased Online now has records from well over 250 cemeteries in Scotland featuring nearly 1.2 million names. Access is by subscription.

Monumental Inscriptions
Little transcription of gravestones has been done in Glasgow. The Glasgow and West of Scotland Family History Society has published a complete index to St David's Ramshorn Burial Ground.

Online Burial Records
The burial records in the Old Parish Registers and the records of St Peter's Dalbeth Cemetery in Glasgow can be searched on the **ScotlandsPeople** website.

Chapter 2

GLASGOW'S HISTORY

EARLY AND MEDIEVAL GLASGOW
Although there is evidence of a fortified prehistoric village on the site and some Roman activity in the area, Glasgow did not begin to develop until the arrival of St Kentigern (also known as St Mungo, c. AD 518 to 603). He came to convert the Britons of Strathclyde to Christianity and founded a church made of wattle and clay near the Molendinar Burn. According to the twelfth-century life of the saint written by Jocelin of Furness, King Rhydderch of Stathclyde had Kentigern consecrated as bishop of a widespread diocese centred on 'a town called Glesgu, which is, interpreted, "The Dear Family", and is now called Glasgu'. Since that date there have been numerous theories as to the origin of the name of Glasgow. During its industrial heyday, *glas* was taken to mean 'grey', leading to such interpretations as 'the grey blacksmith', *gow* suggesting *gobha*, a 'smith'. Today the name is believed to have derived from Glas Ghu meaning 'the dear, green place'.

Kentigern's mother, Teneu, also strongly associated with Glasgow. She is traditionally described as a sixth-century princess of the kingdom of Gododdin (which probably extended from the south-east of Scotland to the north-east of England). She also established a religious community and it is believed that St Enoch Square is today located on the site of a medieval chapel dedicated to her.

Glasgow cathedral now stands on the site of St Kentigern's original foundation to the north-east of the city. Nothing remains of the simple wooden Celtic church or of the Norman church that replaced it. In 1133, John Achaius, Bishop of Glasgow, laid the foundations of a cathedral but it was probably destroyed by fire in about 1176. Bishop Jocelin erected a new cathedral in 1197 of which only a single vaulting shaft in the south aisle of the lower church remains. A third phase was completed during the episcopate of William de Bondington (1233–58) when the East End was remodelled and extended. Major repairs were undertaken in the fifteenth century including the reconstruction of the central tower and chapter house. Thanks to the intervention of the city guilds, it is the only mainland cathedral to have escaped the hands of the religious reformers in the sixteenth century. Today it remains the finest example of pre-Reformation Gothic in Europe, the crypt, with its fan vaulting over the tomb of St Kenigern, being its most notable feature.

Bishop Jocelin, sometime between 1175 and 1178, obtained the royal charter which authorised the creation of a burgh at Glasgow. This gave the tiny settlement the right to hold a weekly market and gave the protection of the king's peace for its inhabitants. Even more importantly, the bishop obtained the town's inclusion within the trade monopoly of 'royal' burghs which permitted legal participation in overseas trade. Nevertheless, it remained a modest town and in 1367, Glasgow was ranked twenty-first of thirty-four burghs taxed.

The seal or signet of Jocelin, Bishop of Glasgow, from Robert Renwick LL.D. and Sir John Lindsay L.D., The History of Glasgow, 3 vols.

During the thirteenth and fourteenth centuries the political influence of Glasgow's bishops secured further royal grants and privileges. In 1451, Glasgow's status was boosted by the foundation of a university (only St Andrews is older in Scotland). It was founded by James II of Scotland who chose the location because it was 'a place of renown and particularly well fitted therefore, where the air is mild, victuals are plentiful, and great store of other things pertaining to man is found'. Classes were first held in the cathedral crypt and the surrounding area until new buildings were established in the High Street, which became the medieval town's main axis.

When the see of Glasgow was raised to an archbishopric in 1492 with authority embracing much of the western Lowlands and southern Highlands, the burgh also gained. The jurisdiction of the episcopal courts was widened and this boosted Glasgow's role as an administrative and judicial centre. Glasgow's foreign trade at this time was probably very slight – European trade was much easier for the burghs on the east coast. Glasgow was essentially a provincial market town, trading principally with its immediate hinterland, the Clyde estuary, Argyll and the inner isles, though even here its position was far from ideal because of the shallows in the Clyde. By 1557, Glasgow had overtaken the other Clyde burghs in its contribution to the National Exchequer but it was still far behind Edinburgh, Dundee, Aberdeen and Perth.

THE REFORMATION AND ITS AFTERMATH

The Reformation Parliament of 1560 passed the laws that laid the foundation of the Protestant Church in Scotland. The new government renounced the authority of the Pope and the propagation of the Catholic faith and celebrating mass was made illegal with severe penalties. Shortly afterwards the first meeting of the General Assembly of the Church of Scotland took place in Edinburgh and the First Book of Discipline was published. These established the Calvinistic doctrine as the basis for the Scottish Protestant Church.

Although the transformation brought about by the Reformation was less violent and protracted in Glasgow than in many parts of the country, the city had grown up under the influence of ecclesiastical rule and with a prominent section of its population belonging to the clerical class. The triumph of Presbyterianism therefore led to considerable confusion as the customs and codes that had prevailed for over 400 years were swept aside. The Crown, the nobles and the great magnates began to transfer the land of the see into their own hands aided by the new Protestant archbishops. These new superiors retained the right to nominate the city's provost and bailies with eminent landowners like the Earl of Lennox, Lord

Boyd, Sir George Elphinston of Blythswood, Thomas Crawford of Jordanhill and Sir Mathew Stewart of Minto occupying the position of chief magistrate for the rest of the sixteenth century.

The Reformation also had serious economic consequences for Glasgow and this was demonstrated by a petition presented to Parliament in 1587 by the freemen and other inhabitants of Glasgow above the Greyfriars Wynd. It stated that their part of the city had, before the Reformation, been 'intertenyt and uphalden' by the resort of the bishop and clergy and had now become ruinous and decayed, and the residents greatly impoverished and without means to keep their property in repair. The petitioners suggested as a remedy that 'the grite confusion and multitude of mercattis togedder in ane place about the croce' should be taken in hand, and some of these markets removed to the upper part of the city. In response the provost and bailies were commissioned to take action by the town council. First, the salt market was removed to a place above the Wynd head; but this was so inconvenient to the fish curers that it was returned to its old position nearer the river, and the bear and malt market was established above the Wynd instead. This petition indicates, not only the straits to which the inhabitants of Glasgow had been reduced, but also that the burgesses had at last realised that they, rather than the Church, were now responsible for the economic prosperity of the city.

From the sixteenth century Glasgow began to develop its overseas trade with Europe and the American colonies. Between 1600 and 1640 the population rose from *c.* 7,000 to *c.* 12,000. Its population was still only a third of Edinburgh's but by 1640 it was around the same size as Dundee and Aberdeen and by 1670 it had overtaken both to become the second most important town in Scotland.

During the Wars of the Covenant of the 1640s Glasgow had to bear its share of levies and taxation. However, it was not pillaged like Dundee and Aberdeen, nor did it suffer repeated increases in taxation, fines and penalties like Edinburgh. Records show that its trade seems to have recovered earlier and more rapidly than that of the other major burghs in the 1650s. Cromwellian Commissioner Thomas Tucker 1655 commented in 1655:

> With the exception of the collegers, all the inhabitants are traders; some to Ireland with small smiddy coals, in open boats, from four to ten tons, from whence they bring hoops, rungs, barrel staves, meal, oats and butter; some to France, with plaidings, coals and herrings, from which the return is salt, pepper, raisins and prunes; some to Norway for timber. There have likewise been some who have ventured as far as Barbados, but the loss which they sustained by being obliged to come home late in the year, has made them discontinue going there any more. The mercantile genius of the people is strong, if they were not checked and kept under by the shallowness of their river, every day more and more increasing and filling up, so that no vessel of any burden can come up nearer the town than fourteen miles, where they must unload and sent up their timber on rafts, and all other commodities by three or four tons of goods at a time, in small cobbles or boats, of three, four or five, and none above six tons a boat.

There were setbacks. In 1649, a dreadful famine and plague all but desolated the town; while in 1652, and again in 1677, it was nearly destroyed by fire. However, Glasgow continued to expand. Hampered by the insufficient depth of water in their old port at Broomielaw, which was accessible only to small craft, the town council took measures for the construction of a new harbour nearer the mouth of the Clyde. They had proposed to form a port at Dumbarton but, after strong opposition from local magistrates, in 1668 they purchased a site on the opposite bank of the river, near the village of Newark, about 19 miles below Glasgow. Trade prospered quickly, and by 1710 Newport Glasgow, later renamed Port Glasgow, had the main Clyde custom house and ships, mostly owned by Glasgow merchants who imported tobacco, sugar, rum, cotton and mahogany from the Americas, as well as timber, iron and

The interior of the Foulis Academy of the Fine Arts in Glasgow University, from Robert Renwick LL.D. and Sir John Lindsay L.D., The History of Glasgow, *3 vols.*

hemp from the Baltic. These goods were then taken by road to Glasgow, as was market-garden produce from farms around Port Glasgow. A change began in 1773 when the Lang Dyke was constructed to deepen the upper river, and ships increasingly went upriver straight to Glasgow.

THE EIGHTEENTH CENTURY

By the beginning of the eighteenth century, Glasgow ranked as Scotland's second city, even though the population of around 15,000 was considerably less than Edinburgh's 35,000. There was a great deal of opposition to the Act of Union in Glasgow where, in 1706, a mob wanting nothing to do with England stormed the council chambers, put the provost to flight and were about to march on Edinburgh when news of the approaching dragoons dispersed them. It is ironic, therefore, that Glasgow was to benefit more than any other Scottish port from the unrestricted access to the colonies for its merchants.

Glasgow's prosperity during the eighteenth century was built upon trade and commerce. By the 1770s they controlled a larger share of the American tobacco trade than all the other ports of the United Kingdom combined. Most of the products were then re-exported to the European mainland, to France in particular. The tobacco merchants, or 'Tobacco Lords' as they are remembered in history, were Scotland's richest trading elite and they invested their wealth in areas such as land, shipping and industry. This stood them in good stead when the colonial trading base was lost as a result of the American War of Independence.

During the later part of the eighteenth century Glasgow's commercial success was built upon the twin foundations of textiles, notably linen and cotton, and iron. Until the 1790s water power was the prime source of energy, but by the nineteenth century the steam-powered mills were able to move to the centres of population and by 1818 there were 18 steam-driven weaving factories in Glasgow with 2,800 looms. The mills were mainly situated in Anderston, Bridgeton and Calton, many employing up to 2,000 people.

The emergence of a factory based textile industry encouraged the growth of a metal working industry relying for many of its components on the Carron Iron Works, near Falkirk, which was established in 1759. Engineering shops were established in Glasgow, principally in Tradeston on the south side of the river and at Camlachie to the east. Ironworks and forges were erected to exploit the ironstone deposits of the Monklands, notably the Clyde Iron Works at Tollcross in 1786. These in turn stimulated demand for coal and men such as James Dunlop and William Dixon built up large colliery enterprises which were later to be integrated with ironworks. Much of the demand for early engineering products came from the textile industry, but during the war with France there was a steady flow of orders for boring cannon and other military equipment. After the American War of Independence a growing number of sailing ships were built at Greenock and Port Glasgow. By the beginning of the nineteenth century the deepening of the river by the Clyde Navigation Trust made it possible for ocean-going ships to reach right into the centre of the city. In 1812 Henry Bell built the *Comet*, the world's first successful passenger steamship, which sailed between Glasgow and Greenock. This helped to usher in the rise of the Clyde's shipbuilding industry, which grew to lead the world and to many came to symbolise the city.

Throughout the eighteenth century Glasgow was noticeably a place of business: it was never an aristocratic city. Dr Alexander Carlyle, a well-known Church of Scotland minister, recalling his student days in Glasgow in the 1740s, lamented the fact that:

> there were only a few families of ancient citizens pretending to be gentlemen, and a few others who were recent settlers there who had obtained wealth and consideration in trade. The rest were shopkeepers and mechanics and successful pedlars, who occupied large ware-rooms full of manufactures of all sorts to furnish a cargo for Virginia. Their manner of life was coarse and vulgar.

Instead it was the Glasgow merchants who made fortunes, which they spent on adopting the lavish lifestyles of aristocrats in their palatial homes. These Tobacco Lords were ostentatious in their black silk breeches, three-cornered hats and red jackets, sporting silver and ebony sticks. Their mansions were laid out on the western boundaries of the eighteenth-century city, where they gave their names to later streets in what is now called the Merchant City section of modern Glasgow. Signs of the construction boom were everywhere. In 1783 Glasgow poet John Mayne boasted:

> Look thro' the town; – the houses here
> Like royal palaces appear.

THE INDUSTRIAL CITY

During the early nineteenth century Glasgow was booming and by 1821 its population had passed that of Edinburgh. By this time there was a prosperous middle class, dominated by businessmen and many well-paid skilled workers in engineering and shipbuilding. Dorothy Wordsworth, in her *Recollections of a tour of Scotland* (1831), was impressed by the outward signs of wealth and prosperity. She was struck by the public buildings and streets:

> which are perhaps as handsome as streets can be, which derive no particular effect from their situation in connexion with natural advantages, such as rivers, sea, or hills. The Trongate, an old street, is very picturesque high houses, with an intermixture of gable fronts towards the street. The New Town is built of fine stone, in the best style of the very best London streets at the West End of the town, but, not being of brick, they are greatly superior.

Dorothy Wordsworth also noticed the lack of aristocratic trappings:

> One thing must strike every stranger in his first walk through Glasgow an appearance of business and bustle, but no coaches or gentlemen's carriages; during all the time we walked in the streets I only saw three carriages, and these were travelling chaises. I also could not but observe a want of cleanliness in the appearance of the lower orders of the people, and a dullness in the dress and outside of the whole mass, as they moved along.

Despite material improvements, the city's fast-growing population put pressure on the supply of food and water. For most people life consisted of poverty and uncertainty. Even those who secured work could find themselves suffering extreme deprivation in times of sickness, in widowhood and especially in old age. As Captain Mills, Superintendent of Police, told a meeting of the British

Association in 1840: 'In the very centre of the city there was an accumulated mass of squalid wretchedness unequalled in any other town in the British Dominions. There was concentrated everything wretched, dissolute, loathsome and pestilential. Dunghills lie in the vicinity of dwellings, and from the extremely defective sewerage filth of every kind constantly accumulate'. Dr J.B. Russell, the Medical Officer of Health for Glasgow, said of the children whose deaths were so numerous in this vile environment:

> Their little bodies are laid on a table or on a dresser so as to be somewhat out of the way of their brothers and sisters, who play and sleep and eat in their ghastly company. From the beginning to rapid-ending the lives of these children are short . . . One in every five of all who are born there never see the end of their first year.

The city's fast-growing population put pressure on the supply of food and water. There were years, notably 1800, when there were riots over shortages of provisions such as oatmeal and potatoes. The town council took steps to ensure the provision of well-regulated and accessible food markets. A notable example from 1818 was the custom-built cattle market in Graham Square, designed to ensure that live animals were no longer sold on the open streets.

Tobias Smollett identified problems with the water as early as 1770, when he commented on the 'hard and brackish' quality of the supply from public wells. Two private water enterprises were established during the 1800s, but these only served districts to the north of the city. Although Glasgow was no stranger to typhus and typhoid, the city's trade connections with the Empire soon brought a new waterborne disease – cholera. The first epidemic in 1832 killed 3,000 in Glasgow, and it returned in 1848 and 1853 in the same overcrowded areas with poor sanitation. It was not until the 1860s that the role of contaminated water in spreading the disease was generally accepted.

The second half of the nineteenth century paved the way for

The Saltmarket from Thomas Annan's The Old Closes and Streets of Glasgow, *created between 1868 and 1871. (University of Glasgow, Special Collections)*

enterprises like slum clearance, gas supply, public lighting, tramways, museums, libraries, art galleries and parks. By the 1890s Glasgow had more municipal services than any other city of its size.

Meanwhile Glasgow's trade and industry grew as did the city boundaries. Robert Gillespie, author of *Glasgow and the Clyde* (1876), lamented the fact that:

> Unfortunately there is no prominent point from which an adequate idea of the size of Glasgow can be gained at a bird's-eye view. The University Tower in early morning, before the smoke from the thousand and one factory chimneys obscures the atmosphere, is perhaps the best post of observation; but even from it the vast extent of Glasgow is scarcely visible. To see the city properly, its streets must be traversed; the East End, with its factories and artisan dwellings; the Centre, with its public institutions, warehouses, offices, and shops; the West End, with the residences of the rich; the Harbour, miles in extent and crowded with shipping, and the river banks for miles below with shipbuilding yards resounding with the harsh clank, clank of the rivetting hammer.

THE LAST ONE-HUNDRED YEARS

By the beginning of the nineteenth century Glasgow had become the industrial capital of Scotland. Glasgow now claimed for herself the title of 'Second City of the Empire', and made, with her satellite towns, one-fifth of the steel, one-third of the railway locomotives and rolling stock, one-third of the shipping tonnage and one-half of the marine-engine horsepower in the United Kingdom. During the First World War, together the Clydeside shipyards were the largest provider of vessels to the Royal Navy, contributing 481 ships between 1914 and 1918. With the loss of so many men to the armed forces, many women joined the workforce. By the end of the war, over 30,000 women were part of Clydeside industries.

After the First World War, Glasgow suffered from the impacts of recession and later the Great Depression which helped fuel the rise of radical socialism. This had already had a major effect on the city in the years before the war. In 1911 alone there were sixty-four strikes. One of the most notable was at the Singer sewing machine

Jamaica Bridge, from Boots Cash Chemists's 'Real Photographic Series'.

factory in Clydebank where 11,000 workers went on strike in March–April 1911 in solidarity with 12 female colleagues protesting against work process reorganisation which involved an increase in workload and a decrease in wages. During the Glasgow Rent Strike of 1915, a popular protest against greedy landlords raising rents on often substandard housing while many breadwinners were on the Western Front dying for their country, the government was forced to intervene and peg rents at pre-war levels.

After a lull, agitation for a shorter working week resulted in a strike called for Monday, 27 January 1919 when more than 40,000 Glasgow workers joined the action. The Clyde Workers Committee – an informal body made up of shop stewards from different trade unions – went to the Glasgow City Chambers to make their case to the Lord Provost. Thousands of their supporters, mostly workers on strike, waited outside in George Square. The sheriff was dispatched to read the Riot Act to the assembled crowd which ended with the police and stikers fighting and this spreading throughout the city, as far east as Glasgow Green, nearly a mile away. An anxious British government, fearing a full socialist revolution, reacted by sending in tanks and placing machine guns on top of high buildings in the city centre. The final official casualty list was nineteen policemen and thirty-four strikers injured and the event was to go down in history as the **'Battle of George Square'** (also known as **'Bloody Friday'** and **'Black Friday'**).

 These events contributed to the changing political complexion of Glasgow and the Clyde after the First World War. Formerly a Liberal stronghold, in 1922 Glasgow returned ten Independent Labour Party MPs (out of a total for the city of fifteen) and it was to remain staunchly Labour for the rest of the century.

The major worldwide economic depression of the 1920s and 1930s set in, particularly affecting the Scottish economy with its dependence on heavy industry and international markets. It was during this period that Glasgow acquired many of the negative stereotypes that were to persist until at least the 1990s. Glasgow Corporation responded with a radical programme of rebuilding and regeneration efforts that started in the mid-1950s and lasted into the late 1970s. This involved the mass demolition of the city's infamous slums and their replacement with large suburban housing estates and tower blocks.

By the late 1980s there had been a significant resurgence in Glasgow's economic fortunes. The 'Glasgow's miles better' campaign, launched in 1983, and opening of the Burrell Collection in 1983 and Scottish Exhibition and Conference Centre in 1985 spearheaded Glasgow's new role as a European centre for business services and finance and promoted an increase in tourism and inward investment. In 2014 more than 2.7 million visitors were attracted to the city making it the fifth most visited city in the United Kingdom. It is only fitting that Glasgow's history plays a major role in attracting tourists with its Gothic cathedral, the Necropolis, the Merchant's House and its countless Victorian structures.

Chapter 3

KEY SOURCES

Scotland is a world leader in providing family history information online. The most useful website is **ScotlandsPeople** (www.scotlandspeople.gov.uk), the official government source of genealogical data for Scotland with almost 90 million records to access. Key sources include births, deaths and marriage records from 1855 to 2006, census records from 1841 to 1911 and indexes of the church baptisms, deaths and burials and marriages that took place between 1538 and 1854, digitised wills and testaments from Scotland's National Archives and Scottish Catholic Archives records. This chapter focuses on these records which will provide the family and local historian with the essential information needed to begin their research.

CENSUS RECORDS

Census records are an obvious place to start research. There has been a census held in Scotland every ten years since 1801 (excluding 1941) but only those returns after 1841 (with a few earlier exceptions) carry details of named residents. The census enumerator would distribute forms to be filled in on census night, and then go from door to door collecting the completed forms: the accuracy of the information is therefore highly dependent upon the head of the household who completed the form.

It is important to remember that ages are not always given correctly on census returns. You may also find that someone is missing from the census return who is known to have been alive at the time. In the case of children, for example, they may have been living with another relative. It is possible that an ancestor was working in some other part of the country on census night, or detained at Her Majesty's pleasure. To add to the confusion, a child may have died in its infancy and a younger child have been given the Christian name of the deceased sibling. What appears to be a mistake in the Christian name of a wife may signify the death of the first wife and a second marriage.

These records do, however, provide invaluable information about family relationships, ages, how ancestors earned their livings and where they were born. Used together with the birth, death and marriage records, they enable the family historian to build a very detailed picture of several generations of ancestors. The census records will give you details of those members of the family who lived at a particular address at the time. They will reveal the age of each member of the family providing you with an important clue to their year of birth which can be followed up in the registration of births. The census returns also detail the rank, profession or occupation of your ancestor and if a person was born in Scotland, the parish of birth was to be stated; if in England, Wales or Ireland, the county; if abroad, the country.

The 1841 Census

It is important to understand that in the 1841 census for those over 15 their exact age was not given, ages being rounded down to the nearest 5 (i.e. those aged between 20 and 25 were all given as 20), presumably for statistical purposes. Missing also from the 1841 census, compared with later ones, are relationships. Families living together are listed together, so it is possible to work out the likely family connection. You may find, however, that persons were not actually related to the head of the family, their 'relation' might be servant, lodger or visitor.

The 1851 and Later Censuses

The 1851 census asked fuller basic questions which were repeated in subsequent censuses. The head of each household had to supply for every person under their roof their Christian names and surname; relation to head of family; 'condition' (married, widowed or unmarried); age; rank, profession or occupation; where born; and whether blind or deaf and dumb. It was not until the 1891 census that the census enquired who spoke Gaelic.

The forms (which were subsequently destroyed) were copied into the enumerator's book, and it is these for 1841 to 1911 that are available to researchers on the **ScotlandsPeople** website. You can also view transcriptions of the 1841–1901 censuses at the subscription sites Ancestry.co.uk, and Findmypast.co.uk.

The **City Archives** also hold the original returns of the 1821 census for Lesmahagow which are available online, http://www.glasgowfamilyhistory.org.uk.

Statistical Publications

After each census there was issued (since 1861 by the Registrar General) a voluminous report containing analysis and statistical tables. These reports were presented to both Houses of Parliament in London and are an invaluable source for the local and social historian. The numerous tables calculated by nation, county, parish and burgh include every possible comparative viewpoint of population, age, occupation, birthplace, houses etc. The information provided to the government on the state of the housing, health, education and occupations of the population is of obvious interest to the social historian. The statistical reports from the censuses from 1801 to 1931 are available at http://www.histpop.org/ohpr/servlet/.

BIRTH, DEATH AND MARRIAGE RECORDS

Registration of births, marriages and deaths began in Scotland on 1 January 1855. All births had to be registered within twenty days, marriages within three days and deaths within eight days. Certificates generally give more information than their English counterparts: for example, death certificates name the parents of the deceased and marriage certificates name mothers as well as fathers of the couple.

Civil registration took the place of the baptism, marriage and burial records entered in the Church of Scotland parish registers, although these events have also continued to be recorded in the registers. Although registration did not take place until 1855, death certificates can extend the family tree well before this date. For instance, if someone who was born in 1790 lived until the grand old age of 75, their death certificate (*c.* 1865) would give two more names to add to the top of the tree, taking things back to a couple born around 1770 or earlier.

Indexes and images of these records canbe found online at **ScotlandsPeople**. Statutory births from 1855 to 1915, statutory marriages from 1855 to 1939 and deaths from 1855 to 1964 are available to view on this site.

Birth Records

Birth records include the date and time of birth; address of where the child was born; gender; father's name and occupation; mother's name and maiden name; date of registration; and informant's name and relationship (if any) to the child. Birth records for 1855 show parents' ages and places of birth; the date and place of the parents' marriage; the number and gender of any children they had already; and whether any of their children had died.

Marriage Records

Until 1929 (when the minimum age was raised to 16) boys could marry at 14 and girls at 12, provided they had parental consent. The marriage records show the names of the bride and groom; occupations of both parties; whether single, widow(er)ed or divorced; ages of both parties; names and addresses of witnesses; names of parents of both parties, including the maiden names of mothers; and name and denomination of the minister. In 1855 alone the records also identified whether either party had been married before, and if so, how many children had been produced and how many of these were still alive. Also, the date and place of birth of the bride and groom were given, and whether these births had been registered.

Illustration from Glasgow's Looking Glass, *1825–6.*

Death Records

Death records show the name; date, time and place of death; cause of death and the name of the doctor if present; occupation; marital status; gender; age; place of death; usual residence, if not the same as the place of death; whether married or widowed; parents' names, including mother's maiden name, and whether the parents were alive or dead; occupation of father; and informant's name and sometimes address. In 1855 and from 1861 onwards you will also find details of the spouse. In 1855 only you will also find details of where the deceased was born and how long they had lived in the place where they died and the names and ages of children born to the deceased.

Key Sources

ADOPTION
Legal adoption was only established in Scotland in 1930. Before 1930 'adoptions' could be arranged by private individuals or by one of a number of charitable adoption agencies or by a Poor Law authority. Since 1930, adoptions have normally been overseen by charitable bodies or local authority 'social work' departments and then ratified by civil courts.

Glasgow City Archives holds the records of the various local authority and predecessor bodies, which were responsible for child care from the middle of the nineteenth century, for Glasgow and for areas of the former Strathclyde Region. The records held by Glasgow City Archives relate to the placement of 'adopted', boarded-out, fostered and in-care children by the following authorities:

- Poor Law authorities that were established in 1845 and acquired responsibility for orphaned, separated or deserted children, including: Glasgow, Bute, Dunbartonshire (West), Lanarkshire (South) and Renfrewshire.
- Glasgow Corporation and Glasgow City Council, 1930–75, 1996–present.
- Strathclyde Regional Council, including records of former county council areas of Argyll, Bute, Dunbartonshire, Lanarkshire and Renfrewshire, 1930–96.

The official birth records and court records of adoptions after 1930 are held by the National Records of Scotland (NRS). There is no general access to these records until 100 years after the child's birth.

WILLS AND TESTAMENTARY RECORDS
Once the date of an ancestor's death has been discovered, it is worth finding out whether they left a will. It is important to remember that there was no legal requirement for individuals to make a will. Even if someone died intestate, there was no obligation for the family to go to court to have the deceased's affairs settled. Many families

The Mercat Cross, 1932. (Postcard published by Valentine & Sons, Ltd, Dundee)

sorted things out amicably among themselves, in which case there will be no testament.

One should not assume that because the family was poor members would not have made a will. Sometimes those who made a will were determined that their money or possessions went to the right person when they died. Strangely it doesn't always follow that people who were in comfortable positions left wills. People from well-to-do families sometimes disposed of their wealth before they died in order to avoid death duties.

Although Scots law can often be radically different to its neighbour south of the border, in terms of wills it worked in quite similar fashion. Wills and testaments provide useful details of what people owned, and to whom they were related. The people generally identified in these records are spouses and children, but you may also find details of parents, brothers, sisters, nieces and nephews, grandchildren and so on.

Key Sources

In Scotland there were also services to heirs (called **retours**). These concerned the inheritance of land held direct from the Crown, and also cases of complicated inheritance, such as grandchildren inheriting from their grandparents because their parents were dead. Retours were also used to appoint 'tutors' or guardians for fatherless children ('pupils').

The Will
A will is a document stating how an individual wants to dispose of their property after their death. The executor of their estate, who is confirmed by a testament approved by the courts, will carry out those wishes.

Testaments
Testaments fell into a further two categories, known as **testament testamentars** and **testament datives**. The former came into effect when the dead person left a will, and had an introduction, an inventory of possessions of the dead person, the will itself (or a copy) and a confirmation clause. Testament datives only applied when no will was left, and were essentially the same as a testament testamentar, except for the will itself. Until the beginning of the nineteenth century, testaments tended to relate only to movable property, but things quickly altered to cover all property.

INHERITANCE
Under Scots law, an individual's property was divided into two types:

- **Heritable property** consisted of land, buildings, minerals and mining rights, and passed to the eldest son according to the law of primogeniture.
- **Moveable property** consisted of anything that could be moved, for example, household and personal effects, investments, tools or machinery. It was divided into a maximum of three parts: the widow's part, the bairns'

part (all children had a right to an equal share) and the dead's part. Before the early years of the nineteenth century, testaments related only to the moveable property of the deceased. However, from the early nineteenth century onwards, it was not uncommon to find dispositions, settlements, trust dispositions and settlements etc. recorded in the commissary court registers, and these documents often included details of heritable property. After 1868, the law of primogeniture, where the eldest son inherited everything, still applied to heritable property unless there had been a specific disposition or bequest by the deceased to another party.

Inventories

The **inventory** lists the moveable property belonging to the deceased at the time of his or her death. It can include household furnishings, clothes, jewellery, books, papers, farm stock and crops, tools and machinery, money in cash, bank accounts and investments, as well as money owed to creditors and money due from debtors. Often the inventory consists only of a brief, overall valuation, but sometimes it is very detailed, with the value of every item listed. As such, it can supply a snapshot of the deceased's lifestyle and help to build up a picture of what social and economic conditions were like in a particular locality at a particular time. An inventory that contains a **roup roll** is particularly interesting in that it itemises each lot sold in the auction and states the prices paid (sometimes with the names of the purchasers).

Probate Records

Glasgow was under the probate jurisdiction of the Commissary Court of Glasgow until 1823, and since then has been under the Sheriff's Court of Glasgow. The Edinburgh Commissary Court, as the principal court, also had the power to confirm testaments for those who owned moveable property in more than one commissariot and for Scots who died outside Scotland.

Key Sources

Finding Wills
Probate records for 1513–1925 are indexed online at www.scotlandspeople.gov.uk. Even an index entry is valuable, offering not only the name of the deceased, but their occupation and where they lived, along with where and when the testament was recorded. Be aware, however, that an index entry won't give you the date of death or what the estate was worth – you'll need a copy of the will itself for that, and you can find images of wills and testaments from 1500 to 1925 on this site for a fee. The early wills for Glasgow have been printed: Francis J. Grant (ed.), *The Commissary Records of Glasgow. Register of Testaments 1547–1800* (1901).

THE OLD PARISH RECORDS
Civil registration in Scotland dates from 1855. Before that date, the registration of baptisms, marriages and burials was the responsibility of the Scottish Church. This information was recorded in the Old Parish Registers (OPRs). Although parishes were ordered to keep registers in 1551, records were often only kept sporadically. In 1829, a survey was sent to seventy-five clergymen and lay pastors throughout the city and suburbs of Glasgow asking for the number of children born or baptised to members of their congregations between 14 December 1829 and 15 December 1830. The returns, considered complete, resulted in a count of 6,397 children. By comparison, only 3,225 children were registered in the parochial registers of the Established Church, which leaves 3,172 children unregistered in that year. This illustrates why many children are not to be found in the OPRs.

Many births and baptisms, proclamations and marriages and burials were not recorded for a variety of reasons. In some cases parents were unwilling to pay to have their children baptised. In other cases the minister or clerk forgot to record an event; registers were incomplete or damaged for periods; families may have fallen out with the minister; or people were members of other religious denominations (for example, Roman Catholics, Free Church, Episcopalians etc.).

For the birth of a child you will usually be given the names of both parents (including maiden name of mother) and often an address and names of witnesses (often relatives). A marriage will sometimes name relatives of the couple. Burial registers usually provide the least information, if they exist at all for the period you need. Evidence of deaths comes from the kirk session records showing payments made for digging the grave or hiring the parish mortcloth (a black cloth draped over the coffin).

Regular marriages were preceded by the proclamation of banns in the parish churches of both parties, with at least two witnesses present. Proclamations were supposed to be made on three consecutive Sundays in order to make public the couple's intention to marry and these proclamations were entered in the OPR. Session clerks seldom bothered recording the date of the wedding itself: if only one date is given this will usually be that of the proclamation. The wedding generally took place within six weeks of the proclamation. The OPR will include the names of the parties and the date of the proclamation. They may also include the parishes of residence, marriage date and the names of witnesses.

If you find two Scottish OPR marriage entries for the same couple on (roughly) the same dates, don't worry about which is yours, they could be one and the same. Banns had to be read in the parish of residence, and if the bride and groom lived in different parishes, the banns had to be read in both parishes so that any objectors to the marriage had a chance to have their say. The banns may not have been read on the same days in both parishes, hence the discrepancy in the dates. It's also a shortcut to finding the possible parishes of birth for each party, or establishing that there were two couples with the same names in the same area.

Marriages not carried out by Church of Scotland ministers or marriages created by people living together without any formal ceremony were known as **irregular marriages**. Until 1834, despite such unions being illegal, the kirk sessions often summoned wrongdoers and fined them before acknowledging the marriage: the union may appear in the OPRs, possibly identified as 'irregular'.

Some irregular marriages were investigated in the law courts, and may turn up in those records.

The **City Archives** hold the records of the original OPRs for the Church of Scotland and those churches which had seceded from the Established Church in the eighteenth and nineteenth centuries, as well as for many other denominations.

CATHOLIC PARISH REGISTERS

Many of the records for Scottish Catholic parishes have been digitally imaged. Copies of these images together with a full index, are one of the many resources available as part of the **ScotlandsPeople** network. Catholic parish registers comprise records of :

- Births and baptisms.
- Marriages.
- Confirmations.
- Deaths and burials.
- Communicants.
- Sick calls.
- Status animarum.
- Converts.
- First confessions.
- Seat rents.

A large number of Catholic parish registers are held in the **Scottish Catholic Archives**. Other records are still retained within the parishes. This is explored in greater detail in Chapter 6.

Chapter 4

LOCAL GOVERNMENT AND TAXATION

THE BURGH AND TOWN COUNCIL
For much of its history Glasgow held the status of a community on the Church lands for which the bishops and archbishops had secured the privileges, successively, of a burgh of barony, a burgh of regality and a royal burgh. For many centuries the day-to-day government of the burgh was in the hands of the burgesses who formed the town council. The office of provost, or chief magistrate, was created in the 1450s. Individuals were nominated for the role of provost and magistrates by the council and approved by the archbishop for the following year. Two of the bailies were chosen from the merchants' guild and one from the crafts. The newly appointed magistrates and those of the two preceding years then met, along with certain co-opted persons, to fill up vacancies, and elected thirteen merchants and twelve craftsmen to be councillors for the year. The town council was therefore a close corporation, nominating its successors, mostly out of its own number.

Although Glasgow became a royal burgh in 1611, directly subject to the Crown, the archbishops continued to control appointments. Ironically, it was at the meeting in Glasgow of the General Assembly of the Church of Scotland in 1638 that an attempt was made to abolish episcopal church governance, setting in motion events that plunged the British Isles into civil war for almost fifteen years. The Presbyterian and Cromwellian governments of the 1640s and 1650s kept a firm grip on the burgh, and the Restoration of the monarchy

Local Government and Taxation

in 1660 brought a full resumption of the archbishops' rights to appoint the town's magistrates.

William of Orange's invasion of England in late 1688 changed everything. The failure of the Scottish bishops to pledge William their support heralded the end of episcopal governance and, in 1690, Glasgow's Town Council finally gained the right to elect the burgh's provost and bailies without Church interference. Having achieved full self-government, the merchants dominated the city for the next 145 years until the Burgh Reform Act of 1833 gave, for the first time, representative government to all royal and parliamentary burghs. A third Act granted extensive powers to the Municipal Police Board, which was responsible for crime fighting, riot-quelling, street lighting, paving, scavenging, water supply, prevention of infectious diseases, bridges and fire prevention. An earlier Municipal Police Board, set up in 1800, had already been granted extensive powers to deal with fire fighting, lighting, street cleansing and later roads and bridges.

GLASGOW CORPORATION

In 1895, the town council formally became the Corporation of the City of Glasgow, and this lasted until 1975 when it became the City of Glasgow District Council. As the corporation, its responsibilies extended to include a wide range of activities including fire protection, bridges, lighting, public health and sanitation, libraries and museums, as well as commercial activities such as water and sewerage, gas, electricity, trams and the Glasgow underground. In 1904 the Police Commissioners duties were transferred. In 1929 the corporation added to these responsibilities education, poor relief and hospitals. By this time it was also responsible for the largest urban tram system in Britain as well as Glasgow's buses and underground.

In 1996, following the dissolution of Strathclyde Regional Council and the transfer of its responsibilities to Glasgow District Council, the authority was renamed Glasgow City Council. The title of Lord Provost, equal in many ways to the role of Mayor, is still elected by the city council to chair that body and to act as a figurehead for the city.

The view from London Street, c. 1910. (Postcard published in the J.M. Caledonia Series)

BURGH RECORDS

A fascinating insight into medieval Glasgow can be found in the Blackhouse charters, which date back to 1304 and are the oldest records held by the **University of Glasgow**. They recount the expansion and relocation of the university over the centuries through Acts of transfer of property, settlements of court, donations and royal grants.

Glasgow's city archives began in *c.* 1175 when Bishop Jocelin obtained a royal charter authorising the bishops to have a burgh at Glasgow. The burgh continued to produce records of its work and maintained these for future reference. In 1560 Archbishop Beaton escaped to Paris and took the records of the burgh with him. He placed them in the Scots College in Paris, and they were taken from there and lost during the French Revolution.

The **Glasgow City Archives** holds copies of some grants and charters made to the city of Glasgow during its earlier history

Local Government and Taxation

(Ref A1); Barony court act books, minutes of burgh commissioners etc., 1700–1900, reference NRA 37295; the records of those admitted as burgesses and freemen for Glasgow, 1573–1969 (incomplete), and for Rutherglen, 1620–1975 (incomplete). For later records and to see the original records of earlier burgess admissions, you can search the burgess roll books and other court records. The main series are detailed below.

Burgesses of the City of Glasgow

- Council minutes, 1573–1609 (Ref. C1/1).
- Dean of Guild act book, 1609–1776 (Ref. B4/1).
- Roll books, 1613–1956 (Ref. C5/1).
- Roll books of Honorary Burgesses of Glasgow, 1800–1969 (Ref. T-TH1/96/2).

Burgesses of Rutherglen

- Burgess registers, 1620–1975 (Ref. RU3/5).

The Charters and Documents Relating to the City of Glasgow 1175–1649, Vols 1 and 2, ed. J.D. Marwick (1897), contains an extensive preface to and commentary on the charters and other documents and transcriptions of 123 key charters and other documents, as well as abstracts of further related documents.

The Scottish Record Society has published lists of burgesses for Glasgow: *The Burgesses & Guild Brethren of Glasgow, 1573–1846*, ed. J.R. Anderson (Scottish Record Society, 1925). The book also gives a detailed description of how you could become a burgess. Also of interest is *Extracts From the Records of the Burgh of Glasgow Vol. 1, 1573–1642*, ed. J.D. Marwick (1876) and *Records of the Burgh of Glasgow* (first edn Scottish Burgh Records Society, Edinburgh, 1914).

RECORDS OF GLASGOW CORPORATION

The archives of Glasgow Corporation and its successor authorities is the largest and most significant collection held in the **Glasgow City Archives** and represents over 400 years of local government in the Glasgow area.

The records include:

- Council minutes dating from 1573.
- Architectural plans: detailed plans of almost every building erected or altered within the city boundaries since 1885.
- School archives: log books and admission registers for over 300 city schools.
- Poor Law archives: records of the various parochial boards in the city and more than 1 million applications for poor relief.
- Annexed burghs: archives of the burghs and other areas annexed to the city in the nineteenth century.

There is also a large quantity of records covering the other functions of the city including fire brigade, housing, transport, police, water supply, health services, licensing, parks, galleries and museums, gas and electricity and telephones.

ELECTORAL RECORDS

Voters' rolls, or electoral registers, list those people eligible to vote in local, parliamentary and other national elections. The Mitchell Library Special Collections and the Glasgow City Archives both hold voters' rolls for Glasgow. In addition the Archives has voters' rolls for areas absorbed into Glasgow as well as for areas of the former Strathclyde Regional Council.

It is important to remember that not everyone had the vote. Only males could vote from 1832 to 1918 in parliamentary elections. Women could vote in municipal elections. Unmarried women and married women, not living with their husband, who were proprietors or tenants, could vote for burgh councillors from 1882 and county councillors from 1889. It was not until 1930 that all men and women over 21 were eligible to vote.

Special Collections has the voters' rolls for Glasgow. These include:

- 1846–current year, parliamentary elections.
- 1872–85, municipal elections, persons living outside the parliamentary boundaries.
- 1898/9, municipal elections, males living outside the parliamentary boundaries.
- 1900–1, municipal elections.
- 1885–92, municipal elections, female voters.

Registers were not compiled for some of the war years: 1915–17 or 1941–4.

In addition to the standard voters' rolls for Glasgow, the **City Archives** also holds the following:

- Glasgow, manuscript volumes, arranged alphabetically, 1833–54.
- Glasgow, absent voters, 1920, which lists names of members of the armed forces.
- Areas absorbed into Glasgow, including: Govan, Hillhead, Kelvindale, Partick and Pollokshaws, municipal and parliamentary elections, 1890s–1912 (incomplete).
- Rutherglen, 1832–1931, 1926 and 1928–36 (part of Glasgow voters' rolls), 1975–96.
- Dunbartonshire, Lanarkshire, Renfrewshire, mainly twentieth century, with occasional early lists of voters as part of family and estate records.

TAXATION

The NRS holds many seventeenth-, eighteenth- and nineteenth-century taxation records for Glasgow. The Hearth and Poll Taxes were levied and the Land Tax began to be collected in the seventeenth century, at a time when Scotland had its own parliament. After the Union of the Parliaments of Scotland and England in 1707, the

View of Stockwell Bridge from the Gorbals side of the River Clyde, 1797.

Window Tax was collected from the mid- to late eighteenth century. You can browse schedules of most of the taxes mentioned below at the subscription based **ScotlandsPlaces website**, www.scotlandsplaces.gov.uk.

Consolidated Schedules of Assessed Taxes, 1798–9

From 1787 taxes were payable to a single consolidated fund. These were entered on a single schedule, which included houses and windows, inhabited houses, male servants, carriages, riding and carriage horses, horses used in husbandry and trade and mules, and dogs. From 1798 onwards the way taxpayers were assessed for these taxes changed, and schedules were drawn up which listed all the taxes due by each taxpayer. Vol. 18 contains the names of tax payers in Lanarkshire from 5 April 1798 to 5 April 1799.

Inhabited House Tax, 1778–98

Duties on inhabited houses were first imposed in 1778. The resulting tax schedules were drawn up by the Exchequer and can be found in voumes 28–32, now held by the NRS (Ref. 326/3/1–65).

Window Tax, 1748–98

From 1748 until 1851 taxes were levied on the occupants of buildings with several windows in Scotland. Window Tax rolls, listing the

Local Government and Taxation

householders and the number of windows in their properties, survive for the period 1748–98 among the records of the Exchequer in the NRS (Ref. E326/1). The Window Tax had been imposed in England from 1696. The names of those who paid Window Tax in Glasgow between May 1753 and May 1759 are found in vols 172–81 and 218.

Horse Tax Rolls, 1785–98

These volumes provide information on those who paid taxes on carriage and saddle horses in the late eighteenth century in the Scottish counties and royal burghs between 1785 and 1798. Vols 3, 5, 8, 11, 14, 16, 19, 22, 25, 28, 31 and 33 contain information on the burgh of Glasgow.

Carriage Tax Rolls, 1785–98

Between 1785 and 1798 the owners of two- or four-wheeled carriages in Scotland paid tax on their carriages. In Carriage Tax rolls you will find the names of carriage owners and the types of carriage they owned, as well as the duty paid in tax. Vols 2, 4, 7, 10, 12, 14, 16, 18 and 20 are for Glasgow.

Cart Tax Rolls, 1785–98

Between 1785 and 1798 the owners of two-, three- or four-wheeled carts in Scotland were taxed. The tax fell mainly on farmers and landowners in the rural areas and carters in the towns. Cart Tax rolls list the names of cart owners and the types of cart they owned, as well as the duty paid in tax. Volumes 2, 3, 5, 7, 9, 11 and 13 are for Glasgow.

Hearth Tax Rolls

Hearth Tax rolls list the people who were liable for tax on hearths (including kilns) in Scotland in the 1690s. They provide clues about the size of each building, place, estate or parish in the late seventeenth century. Heads of households of each building were liable for a tax of 14s, payable at Candlemas 1691, and only hospitals and the poor were exempt. The surviving Hearth Tax rolls

(NRS Ref. E69) are generally arranged by county and then parish or by landed estate. Hearth Tax records for Lanarkshire, Vol. 1 contains a list of householders liable for Hearth Tax in Lanarkshire in 1694.

Female Servant Tax Rolls, 1785–92
In Scotland, taxes were levied on households employing 'non-essential' female servants between 1785 and 1792. Most of the servants listed were engaged in domestic work. The tax schedules (NRS, Ref. E326/6) cover the years 1785–92 and the rolls for the burgh of Glasgow can be found in vols 4, 8, 12, 16, 20, 24 and 28.

Male Servant Tax Tolls, 1777–98
The Male Servant Tax was levied on the households employing 'non-essential' male servants from 1777 onwards. This excluded farm labourers, industrial workers and servants in businesses like shops and inns. The tax was aimed primarily at the wealthy in the town and country who could afford domestic or personal servants (such as cooks, butlers, valets, grooms, gardeners and coachmen). The tax schedules (NRS, Ref. E326/5) cover the years 1777–9, 1785–95 and 1797–8 and the tax rolls for burgh of Glasgow can be found in vols 2, 4, 6, 8, 10, 12, 14, 16, 18, 20, 22, 24 and 26.

Farm Horse Tax Rolls, 1797–8
The Farm Horse Tax rolls (NRS, Ref. E326/10) list the names of the owners and numbers of horses and mules used in husbandry or trade in 1797–8. In some rolls the tax inspectors made repeat visits to track down non-payers, which explains why some parishes and burghs are repeated; vols 4 and 10 Lanarkshire, vols 6 and 13 Burgh of Glasgow.

Poll Tax, Lanarkshire, 1694–8
Poll taxes were imposed in 1694, 1695 and twice in 1698 to pay off the debts and arrears of the army and navy. The barony parish of Glasgow and the parishes of Govan and Cadder can be located on the ScotlandsPlaces website.

Chapter 5

LAND AND PROPERTY OWNERSHIP

Glasgow was established on the land of a dozen or so landowners who had been established on their estates for centuries. To the south-west stood the estates of the Houldsworths, the Andersons of Stobcross and, at Yorkhill, of Mrs Glibert Graham. West of this, and still beyond the county boundaries, were the estates of the Oswalds, Dowanhill, the Gilmorehill Company (later acquired by the University of Glasgow), Hillhead and what was to become the Kelvinside Estate Company. To the east were the holdings of the Glasgow Building Company, Glasgow University and beyond that Dennistoun Estate, originally owned by cotton merchant Richard Dennistoun before being acquired by another merchant, Colin McNaughton. South of the river lay the Maxwell estate, the district of Tradeston, owned largely by the Trades' House of Glasgow (consisting of the fifteen individual craft incorporations within the city), and to the west of that the area owned by Hutcheson's Hospital. The village of Gorbals was by this time the property of Glasgow Town Council.

Glasgow's rapid expansion during the nineteenth century saw the break-up of these large estates as the city expanded its boundaries into what where still substantially rural areas in the 1870s. One such was the 470-acre Blythswood Estate upon which a large part of west Glasgow now stands. Purchased around 1670 by Provost Colin Campbell, the estate extended westward from what are now called Mitchell and West Nile Streets, along the north side of Argyle Street and Dumbarton Road and in the process gave its name to the Blythswood Square.

The Scotstoun Estate, until the early 1860s owned by the Oswald family, contained about 1,000 acres and stretched from the River Clyde to Great Western Road. It included not only the districts which we now know as Scotstoun and Whiteinch, but also Claythorn (Whittingehame Drive area) and lands around the former Knightswood Hospital. By 1861 the westward expansion of the Clyde shipbuilding yards had reached Scotstoun with the opening of the Charles Connell and Company shipyard in 1861 and the new Yarrow Shipbuilders yard in 1906. This led to the break-up of the estate, as portions were sold off for housing, to create Victoria Park and for further industrial development (iron, engineering and shipbuilding) along the river, with companies such as the Coventry Ordnance Works and Albion Motors locating in the area.

The Maxwells were substantial landowners south of the Clyde. Pollokshields was developed in the middle of the nineteenth century to a plan promoted by the Stirling Maxwells of Pollok, whose association with the area went back as far back as 1270. The new suburb was designed to accommodate middle-class Glaswegians seeking quality housing beyond the boundaries of the congested city. In 1934 as part of a plan to re-house people from Glasgow's slums, Glasgow Corporation purchased land from Sir John Stirling Maxwell (1886–1956) to build a housing estate. Maxwell laid down stringent conditions on the form the estate must take, resulting in what is today called Old Pollok. The houses with gardens, three bedrooms, separate kitchen and toilet were a vast change from the overcrowded tenements of Glasgow from which most of the new residents came.

The lands at Anderston had been given to the Bishop of Glasgow by King James II of Scotland in 1640. Named after James Anderson of Stobcross House, it changed from farm lands to weaving cottages and then became a major cotton centre. In the process it swallowed up the estates of Lancefield and Hydepark. Finnieston, a small village west of Anderston, was named after the Orr family tutor, the Revd John Finnie. This was the home of the Verreville pottery and an

Robert Paul, A View of Glasgow from the South West, *1764, facsimile of an engraving.*

early producer of fine crystal. The Robert Fulton Alexander Estate became Yorkhill basin, the Children's Hospital and the area through which now runs the Clydeside Expressway.

By the latter half of the nineteenth century the largest single group, in terms of the size of holdings, was the railway companies (12 per cent of the city). The Caledonian Railway Company was the largest owner of this group with city centre property acquired in advance of its Central station development. The next two most substantial groups were private and institutional trusts who owned just over 11 per cent. The three largest were held on behalf of individuals, George Wilson, William Dixon and J.H. Gray. The Glasgow Corporation, with 176 acres within the city boundary, was second only to the Caledonian Railway Company in terms of ownership. This was mostly accounted for by Glasgow Green and West End Park.

LANDED ESTATE RECORDS

The **Glasgow City Archives** holds a large number of collections of family and estate papers for areas across a sizeable part of Scotland. The following lists just some of the collections:

- Blythswood Estate, Glasgow and Renfrew, 1662–twentieth century.
- Campbell of Succoth and Garscube, Glasgow and Dunbartonshire, 1533–1965.
- Colquhoun of Luss, Dunbartonshire, 1188–twentieth century.
- Cochrane-Baillie of Lamington, Lanarkshire, nineteenth–twentieth century.
- Crum Family Papers, Thornliebank, Renfrewshire, 1782–1960.
- Hamilton Family of Barns, Old Kilpatrick, Dunbartonshire, 1537–1827.
- Houston of Johnstone, Renfrewshire, 1664–1951.
- Islay Estate, Islay, Argyllshire, 1741–1966.
- Lennox Family of Woodhead, Dunbartonshire, 1421–1960.
- Maxwells of Pollok, Glasgow and Renfrew, *c.* 1200–1975.
- Ramsay of Kildalton, Islay, Argyllshire, 1707–1984.
- Speirs of Elderslie, Renfrewshire and Dunbartonshire, 1561–1999.
- Stirling of Keir and Cadder, Dunbartonshire and Perthshire, 1338–*c.* 1940s.

Glasgow University Archives holds later records for the Garscube estate, GB 248 DC/080.

LOCATING RECORDS
Tracking down surviving records for a particular locality is largely a matter of finding out the name of the landowner of the day and then checking the indexes and catalogues in different archives to see if any of his records survive. By far the most convenient source for the study of landownership in Glasgow at this time are the **parliamentary**

Land and Property Ownership

returns of 1872 and 1873 which recorded details of all owners of land of one or more areas in England, Wales and Scotland. The returns were collected by county; burghs with a population of over 20,000 were enumerated separately. The returns for Glasgow accounted for the ownership of just less than 4,800 acres of land, not including rivers, canals and quarries. These 4,800 acres were owned by just 2,000 individuals, 1,600 owning less than 1 acre.

You may already know the name of the local landowner, in which case you should consult the National Register of Archives maintained by The National Archives: Historical Manuscripts Commission (TNA) and the Scottish Archive Network (SCAN) online catalogue, http://www.nationalarchives.gov.uk/nra/default.asp.

It may also be relevant to consult the NRS electronic catalogue at http://www.NRS.gov.uk/catalogues/default.asp (most of the estate records in the NRS are part of the Gifts and Deposits (NRS Ref. GD) series).

If you do not know the identity of the landowner(s) in a particular area, there are several publications that can aid you. These publications, as well as others, should be available through a good library, as well as being available for consultation at the Mitchell Library:

- *Ordnance Survey Gazetteer*, 6 vols by Francis H. Groome (Edinburgh, 1883).
- *Statistical Account of Scotland*, 3 Series, numerous volumes compiled by the ministers of the Church of Scotland, various editors (Edinburgh, 1791–9, 1845 and 1987).
- *A Directory of Landownership in Scotland c 1770*, ed. Loretta R. Timperley (Edinburgh, Scottish Record Society, 1976).

REGISTER OF SASINES

The word 'sasine', which shares the same root as the English word 'seize', refers in Scots law to the transfer of what is known as 'heritable property', primarily land and buildings, but also other, geographically fixed, items such as mineral rights (fundamentally important in parts of Scotland from the eighteenth century onwards) and fishing rights.

In Scots' law the sale of land was conducted before witnesses and recorded in notaries' protocol books. It will normally detail the names of the new and previous owners and will give a basic description of the property transferred. There will usually be an indication of the price paid for the property.

The Register of Sasines is Scotland's property register from 1617. Before this date, property transfers were recorded in notarial protocol books. From 1681 there were also separate registers for about seventy royal burghs including Glasgow.

The City Archives holds:

- Glasgow Burgh Register of Sasines, 1694–1927 (B10/26).
- Glasgow Town Clerk's protocol books, 1547–1696 (B10/1).
- Minute books of Rutherglen Burgh Register of Sasines, 1839–1938 (RU2/9).

From 1781 onwards, there were printed abridgements of sasines, covering the Particular and General Registers (the latter was abandoned in 1868). Abridgements of Sasines, 1781–1980s, including indexes, for the Strathclyde area:

- Argyll.
- Ayrshire.
- Bute.
- Dunbartonshire.
- Glasgow, Barony and Regality.
- Lanarkshire.
- Renfrewshire.

The Glasgow Town Clerk's protocol books have been printed in R. Renwick, *Abstracts of Protocols of the Town Clerks of Glasgow 1547–1600* (1894).

Land and Property Ownership

VALUATION RECORDS

In 1855 a new system of valuation began in Scotland, which introduced annual rolls for the tax on property in every burgh and county in Scotland. These include rateable commercial and domestic property in Glasgow. Rates on domestic property ceased in 1988 with the introduction of the council tax. The valuation rolls give the names of the proprietor and tenants. Tenants' occupations were normally given until 1918, and were recorded less consistently thereafter until they disappeared in about 1957/8.

The City Archives holds the annual valuation for the following areas:

- Glasgow, 1855–1912 (samples only, though good for burghs such as Govan, Pollokshaws etc.), 1913/14–1987/88.
- Rutherglen, 1863–4, 1914–15, 1929/30–1971/2 (Glasgow from 1975).
- Lanarkshire, 1855–72, 1894–5, 1975–90.
- Renfrewshire, 1907–84.

Special Collections holds valuation rolls from 1953/4–2010. The valuation rolls for 1855–6 to 1930 have been digitised and are available on the **ScotlandsPeople website**.

Early Valuation Rolls

The City Archives have a number of earlier valuation rolls, variously called assessment, cess or stent rolls, for towns and country areas. These include county valuations for the following areas:

- Argyllshire, 1751.
- Ayrshire, 1705–1975.
- Buteshire, 1771.
- Dunbartonshire, *c.* 1779, 1811–25, 1872–3, 1840.
- Lanarkshire, 1722, 1738, 1747–1872, 1837, 1894–5.
- Renfrewshire, 1654, 1735, 1746.

DEEDS

A deed is a legal agreement, obligation or other document registered with a court in order to establish the basis of a legal right before proceeding to a related legal action. In registering the deed, the person presenting it paid a fee to a court clerk who copied the document into the register and then kept the original document. This original document was called the warrant. While for most genealogical purposes the recorded version is satisfactory, the warrant will show the signatures of the parties to the deed.

In copying the document, many clerks also made a brief note of the entry in a separate minute book. These were kept to prove that they had done their work but they were also used as an index if records had to be retrieved. Modern searchers can use them in the same way. Once registered, the parties received certified extracts of the document.

The Deeds for Glasgow were registered by royal burgh courts. The City Archives hold the Burgh Register of Deeds for Glasgow, 1622–1955 (B10/10/10-16). Occasionally, wills and codicils (additions to wills) that cannot be found in the court records in Edinburgh can be found in the Registers of Deeds.

Chapter 6

THE CHURCH IN GLASGOW

Today Glasgow is a city of significant religious diversity. The city has four Christian cathedrals: Glasgow cathedral (Church of Scotland); St Andrew's Cathedral (Roman Catholic Church); St Mary's Cathedral (Scottish Episcopal Church); and St Luke's Cathedral (Greek Orthodox Church). The Sikh community is served by four gurdwaras and a Hindu mandir. Glasgow Central Mosque in the Gorbals district is the largest mosque in Scotland and, along with twelve other mosques in the city, caters for the city's Muslim population. This is very different from the situation a century ago. Religious divisions in the city were a feature for much of the nineteenth and twentieth centuries. Protestant and Catholic children generally went to separate schools, lived in different streets and areas of the city and this rivalry was played out on the football field between Rangers from the west of the city and Celtic in the east.

For much of its history after the Reformation, Glasgow has been a predominately Presbyterian city. The Scottish Reformation swept aside Scottish Catholicism which five centuries earlier had been declared 'a special daughter' of the Roman see, subject only to the Pope. All manifestations of the old church were obliterated: monasteries and bishops, clerical vestments, holy relics and market-square crosses. Glasgow cathedral was spared thanks to the intervention of the city guilds and today remains the finest example of pre-Reformation Gothic architecture in Europe.

By the middle of the eighteenth century Presbyterianism was in a comfortable ascendancy in Glasgow. The Kirk session was the local court for all manner of minor civil as well as religious offences (ranging from Sabbath desecration and fornication to assault, wife-beating and infanticide). It was the collector and distributor of poor relief and issued 'testimonials' to allow migrants to be received in other parishes. The parish school was designed to educate all children, and the kirkyard was usually the only place for burials.

The chief characteristic of the Scots which made the biggest impression on many travellers from south of the border was, in the words of John Macky in 1723, 'their religious soberness and decorous observance of the Sabbath'. He noted that 'there is nothing of the gaiety of the English, but a sedate gravity on every face, without the stiffness of the Spaniards; and I take this to be owing to their praying and frequent long graces which gives their looks a religious cast'. The Reformation Sabbath began at 6 o'clock in the evening of Saturday and lasted for 24 hours. During this time there was to be no work done, no unseemly activities, no dancing, no playing of the pipes, no markets or frequenting of alehouses. Kirk sessions arraigned women for selling candles and bread on the Sabbath, a miller for grinding corn and a poultry man for plucking geese. Sabbath-keeping according to H.G. Graham, in *Social Life of Scotland in the Eighteenth Century*, was rigorously enforced in Glasgow:

> To secure proper observance of the Sabbath, compurgators, or 'bumbailies', patrolled the streets and wynds on Saturday night to see that by ten o'clock all folk were quietly at home; and if incautious sounds betokening untimely revelry issued from behind a door, or a stream of light from chinks of a window-shutter betrayed a jovial company within, they entered and broke up the party which dared to be happy so near the Lord's own day. On Sabbath, as in other towns, the seizers or elders, in their turn, perambulated the streets during divine service, and visited the Green in the evening, haling all 'vaguers' to kirk or session. The profound stillness of the Sabbath was preternatural, except when the multitudinous tramp of heavy shoes came from a vast voiceless throng of

churchgoers. In these streets of which the patrols 'made a solitude and called it peace', at all other hours no persons passed, no sound was heard, no dog dared bark. In the mirk Sabbath nights no lamp was lit, because all but profane persons were engaged in solemn exercises at home. During the day the window-shutters were, in strict households, just opened enough to let inmates see to walk about the room, or to read the Bible by sitting close to the window-panes.

Those who were not members of the Kirk could find life difficult as George Fox, the founder of Quakerism, discovered when he visited Glasgow in 1657:

I went to Glasgow, where a meeting was appointed; but not one of the town came to it. As I went into the city the guard at the gates took me before the governor, who was a moderate man. Much discourse I had with him; but he was too light to receive the truth, yet he set me at liberty; so I passed to the meeting. But seeing none of the town's-people came to the meeting, we declared Truth through the town; then passed away, visited Friends' meetings thereabouts . . .

Despite the dominate position enjoyed by the Kirk, the eighteenth century saw deep divisions develop within the Church. Two pieces of legislation passed in 1712 proved to be particularly controversial. One granted religious toleration to the Episcopalians. The other removed the system under which ministers were appointed by all the heritors and elders of a parish and restored an earlier system whereby they were nominated by a single patron, in the case of Glasgow this was the town council. This led to problems when, after 1730, patrons tried to install ministers who were not approved of by the majority of their congregations.

A further cause for grievance was the system of pew-renting, which had existed in most Glasgow churches since the mid-seventeenth century and had traditionally been used to provide rich

The cathedral and Royal Infirmary, 1907 or earlier. (Postcard by E.A. Schwerdtfeger & Co., London E.C.)

and poor with access to places of worship. Glasgow Town Council, which owned and managed nearly all the Established churches in the city up to the 1810s, had until the 1780s allocated free church seats to the very poor, reserved large numbers of 'low-rented' seats (under 2s. 6d. per annum) for the 'lower classes of inhabitants' and set aside pews for the inmates of city pauper institutions. At the other end of the social scale, seats were allocated to university staff, students, the town council and members of the incorporated trades; some seats were owned by wealthy families, and some seats were rented to individuals by virtue of long-standing family tradition. Only after all these seats were distributed were the remainder rented out, often by 'roup' (auction).

In Glasgow between 1782 and 1812, there were large and repeated rent increases as demand rose with population increase, and low-rented and free seats were removed or made available for renting to the highest bidder. The system spread across all denominations (with the partial exception of the Baptists) and to every part of the country in the late eighteenth century. This was the reason for much of the non-church going by unskilled and lower paid workers. The Glasgow City Mission, in its first annual report of 1827, noted that a quarter of all the seats in the city's churches were empty, and identified the main cause as the high level of pew rents. It also noted that the need for fine clothes to attend church was beyond the means of the poor.

After years of growing discontent, over a third of the clergy of the Church of Scotland signed a Deed of Demission in 1843, left their manses and formed their own church, the Free Church of Scotland under the leadership of Thomas Chalmers, minister of the Tron Church and St John's in Glasgow. This event, remembered as 'The Great Disruption', led seceding ministers to turn their backs on a secure income and made them dependent on the financial support of their new congregation.

ROMAN CATHOLICISM

By the nineteenth century, the Roman Catholic Church was also gaining ground for the first time since the Reformation. The Jacobite risings in 1715 and 1745 had damaged the Catholic cause in Scotland and it was not until the start of Catholic Emancipation in 1793 that Roman Catholicism regained a measure of respectability. In the 1770s, priests travelled from Perth and Edinburgh to minister to the twenty or so Catholics in Glasgow, and in the 1790s priests migrated with their Highland flocks to the city and its environs. In 1797 a small chapel was built in Marshall Lane, opposite the Barracks, with accommodation for up to 600 worshippers.

The influx of immigrants to Glasgow from Ireland and the Highlands led to a rapid increase in numbers and by the 1830s Catholics made up about 13 per cent of Glasgow's population, with higher concentrations developing in nearby industrial districts like Old Kirkpatrick, Renfrewshire and Monklands. In 1814 work began on a new chapel in Clyde Street on a prominent riverside site which was completed in 1817 and could hold over 2,000 people. It was the focal point for Roman Catholic worship in Glasgow and the west of Scotland and became a cathedral in 1889. Roman Catholicism is today practised by 27.3 per cent of the city of Glasgow.

EPISCOPALIANS

After the Reformation the national church vacillated between Episcopalians and Presbyterianism for over a century before finally declaring Scotland Presbyterian, with the Church of Scotland receiving all church buildings and assets. In 1689 the Scottish Episcopal Church originated with those who refused to accept the Revolution Settlement. It suffered because of its continued allegiance to the Stuart dynasty and was persecuted for the next century. The remnants of these 'Scotch' Episcopalian 'non-jurors' (i.e. those who would not swear their allengiance to a Hanoverian monarch) were treated with great suspicion. Episcopal clergymen ministering to English congregations in Scotland were known as 'jurors'. But the beginning of the nineteenth century saw the laws against Episcopalians relaxed; the increased trade and cultural links between Scotland and England encouraged growth in the church. In 1750 St Andrew's-by-the-Green was built by public subscription to minister to the English community in Glasgow. In 1805 the two branches of the church, the jurors and non-jurors, came together under William Abernethy Drummond, Bishop of Glasgow.

BAPTISTS

The earliest record of Baptists in Glasgow dates from 1770 when Archibald McLean, printer and bookseller, brought together a congregation which met in a house in the High Street. These early Baptists were called 'Scotch' Baptists to distinguish them from their English counterparts. By the 1860s there were seven Baptist meeting places in the city (three Scotch and four English) but their numbers remained small until the First World War, when there were twenty-seven churches mainly in suburbs such as Queen's Park, Hillhead, Partick and Maryhill. From the 1920s Baptist numbers started to decline and by the Second World War many churches had moved

The Black Stool *by David Allan (1744–96). A young bachelor is accused of fornication.*

out of the city and closed. There are now some twenty churches in the Glasgow area.

METHODISTS
Although John Wesley visited Glasgow many times there was no permanent Methodist Society in the city until 1765. The first society met in a room in the Barbers' Hall in Stockwell Street for the next twenty years until new chapels were opened in John Street (1787) and Bridge Street, Tradeston (1813), Great Hamilton Street (1817), Anderston and Parkhead. Thereafter their numbers declined and they were forced to sell the Great Hamilton Street building to the town council in 1820 which became St James's Parish Church. Their current handbook lists three stations only in the Glasgow area.

QUAKERS
George Fox established a small society in Glasgow in 1657. In spite of much hostility from the authorities, they founded a meeting house somewhere off the Trongate which was superseded in about 1730 by a building in Stirling Square, between High Street, Ingram Street and Albion Street. Because of dwindling membership this building was sold in 1791, and the proceeds used to build a Meeting House at the Pleasance in Edinburgh. In Partick there is a tiny burial ground which was used by Quakers in Glasgow from 1711–1857. It is located just off Keith Street.

By 1815 the Glasgow Meeting had revived sufficiently to get its third permanent building in North Portland Street, on the site now occupied by the Livingstone Tower of Strathclyde University. This was abandoned in 1921 and the Meeting was held in the Literary and Philosophical Society in Bath Street until 1944, when the house at 16 Newton Terrace was purchased, and furnished with the benches from the abandoned Pleasance Meeting House.

By the late 1990s Newton Terrace could not accommodate the increased size of the Meeting and it was sold in 1991 and the Friends moved to temporary premises while the search for a new property continued. After considering thirty possibilities the Royal Artillery Club premises at 38 Elmbank Crescent were purchased early in 1992.

CHURCH RECORDS
Church of Scotland
For above 300 years before the introduction of civil registration in Scotland in 1855, the Church of Scotland recorded baptisms, marriages and burials within its parish registers, and it continues to do so. This information was recorded in the **OPRs**. You can see what OPR material survives by consulting the List of the Old Parochial Registers of Scotland at www.scotlandspeoplehub.gov.uk/research/list-of-oprs.html. The OPR is explored in greater detail in **Chapter 3, Key Sources**.

The Glasgow City Archive holds the original records for Glasgow Presbytery and its parish churches from the sixteenth to the twentieth centuries. These comprise the records of churches which are now Church of Scotland, including former seceding churches. The records of the individual parishes include:

- Minutes of Kirk sessions which dealt with discipline cases, including cases of illegitimacy and irregular marriage.
- Registers of baptisms, marriages and proclamations, and (occasionally) burials, including pre-1855 registers for a number of seceding churches.
- Communion rolls, sometimes pre-1855.
- Membership rolls and other lists of parishioners, sometimes pre-1855.

Often the only record that a death has taken place may be the payment of a fee to the parish for the hire of a mortcloth which was draped over the coffin or the corpse for the funeral. This may be found in parish financial records.

The City Archives holds the archives of the large number of seceding churches which previously split from the Established Church from the eighteenth to nineteenth centuries, before reuniting with it in the twentieth century.

Established Church Kirk Session Records	
Church	Records
St Mungo's	Minutes, 3 November 1583, 29 March 1593, 28 November 1583, October 1592 North Session Minutes, 1788–1975 CH2/550 Poor relief distributions, 1788–97 Poor relief distributions, 1797–1809, 1798–1809

	Poor relief distributions, 1809–16 List of elders, 1779–1832, 1809–34 CH2/550/7 High church minutes, 1870–86 CH2/550/8 Minutes of General Session, 1782–95
Tron	CH2/594 Records of Tron Kirk Session, Glasgow, 1788–1925 CH2/594/1 Minutes, 1788–98 Poor accounts, 1788–98, 1788–98
Alford	CH2/9 Minutes, 1717–1809, 1873–1952 Poor Fund, 1842–55
Down	CH2/1052 Minutes and accounts, 1769–85 CH2/1052 Records of Down (later Macduff) Kirk Session, 1769–1933 CH2/1052/3 Baptismal register, 1859–85
St George's West Parish	CH2/818 Minutes, 1771–80, 1812–1913 Poor Fund Debursements, 1784–98 Roll book, 1792–1818, 1823
Calton	CH2/725 Managers' minutes, 1823–51 Cash book, 1791–1955
Brownfield Chapel	CH2/643 Minutes, 1839–48
Laurieston	CH2/1216 Minutes, 1850–81
Martyrs	CH2/999 Collection book, 1852–1946

St John's	CH2/176 Various minutes, 1819–40, 1848–1938 Records of Glasgow, St John's Kirk session, 1819–98 CH2/176/7 Baptismal register, 1897–1963
Shettleston	CH2/178 Managers' Minutes, 1825–1903 Accounts, 1833–91 Seat Rent Accounts, 1779–1853
St Thomas's	CH2/635 Minutes, 1834–43 Cash book, 1851–74
St Peter's	CH2/665 Various minutes, 1849–1946 Marriage register, 1849–1901 Communion roll, 1850–8 CH2/665/6 Baptismal register, 1866–96 CH2/665/7 Baptismal register, 1897–1946 CH2/665/8 Marriage register, 1849–1901, 1849–1933 CH2/665/9 Proclamation register, 1935–47 CH2/665/10-13 Communion roll, 1849–1950 CH2/665/14 Marriage register, 1906–51
St Mark's	CH2/177 Managers' minutes, 1850–64
St Matthew's	CH2/645 Minutes, 1852–82
Springburn	CH2/774 Minutes 1854–1966
Stockwell	CH2/519 Constitution of Church, 1837 CH3/954 Minutes, 1842–43

Roman Catholic Church

Approximately 700 registers have survived, the earliest dating from 1703, but most records only begin in the 30 years following the relaxation of legislation against Catholics in the 1790s. The records cover all Scottish parishes in existence by 1855 – before the introduction of civil registration. They also include the records of the main Catholic cemeteries in Glasgow and the records of the RC Bishopric of the Forces, which records all sacramental events for British men and women serving in the armed forces worldwide.

Many of the records for Scottish Catholic parishes, together with some Catholic cemetery records, have been digitally imaged and are available as part of the **ScotlandsPeople** network.

A large number of Catholic parish registers are held in the **Scottish Catholic Archives** as follows:

Catholic Church Parish Registers			
Diocese	Mission	Parish	Dates
MP/73	Barrhead, St John's	Glasgow	1841–1961
MP/71	Dumbarton, St Patrick's	Glasgow	1830–42
MP/63	Duntocher, St Mary's	Glasgow	1841–1967
MP/69	Glasgow, Immaculate Conception	Glasgow	1849–1921
MP/72	Glasgow, St Aloysius'	Glasgow	1854–1995
MP/64	Glasgow, St Alphonsus'	Glasgow	1847–84
MP/62	Glasgow, St Andrew's	Glasgow	1795–1869
MP/92	Glasgow, St John's	Glasgow	1846–85
MP/65	Glasgow, St Joseph's	Glasgow	1850–1920
MP/70	Glasgow, St Mary Immaculate	Glasgow	1849–1927
MP/66	Glasgow, St Mary's	Glasgow	1842–56
MP/67	Glasgow, St Mungo's	Glasgow	1851–78
MP/68	Glasgow, St Patrick's	Glasgow	1850–86
MP/96	Glasgow, St Paul's	Glasgow	1851–86

Nonconformist Records

The City Archives is also the approved repository for the records of the Episcopal Diocese of Glasgow and Galloway. These include the administrative records of the diocese itself but also the records of a number of churches, mainly from Glasgow and its immediate surroundings. As is the case with the Presbyterian dissenting churches, these also include baptismal, marriage and other records for before 1855, which supplement the OPRs. Among them are the archives of St Andrews-by-the-Green which have baptismal and other registers dating from the eighteenth century; this church baptised large numbers of Irish, troops and residents of other parishes.

The Archives hold the records of many other denominations. These include records of the Evangelical Union and Congregational Churches from throughout Scotland. There are also a number of archives for Methodists churches and of a major Baptist church. For details of the City Archive holdings visit the continually updated FamilySearch website at https://familysearch.org/wiki/en/Glasgow,_Lanarkshire,_Scotland#Church_Records.

Chapter 7

TRADE AND INDUSTRY

It was during the seventeenth and eighteenth centuries that Glasgow transformed from a modest cathedral town into a busy commercial centre. Glasgow had been known for centuries for the curing of Clyde salmon and herrings, which were exported to France and Holland in return for brandy, wines and salt. As markets opened up Glasgow prospered and it was the trade in tobacco, sugar, rum and cotton which would lead to an unprecedented growth in the prosperity of the town. Defoe, in his tour through Scotland in 1723, says that twenty or thirty ships came there every year from the plantations with tobacco and sugar, and later, in the edition of 1727, he says, 'they now send near fifty sail of ships every year to Virginia, New England, and other English colonies in America'. He points out the great advantage Glasgow had over London because the ships did not have to go down the Channel, so that they were often 'at the Capes of Virginia before the London ships got clear of the Channel, and thus saved a month or six weeks on the whole voyage'.

The merchants built large ships specifically for the American tobacco trade and developed personal networks in the New World, particularly in Virginia on the east coast.

From the 1750s onwards, the Clyde was handling a larger share of Europe's tobacco than all the British ports combined. At the end of the American War of Independence the newly founded American Republic began to trade directly with Europe on its own. Glasgow's tobacco merchants soon dwindled with many going out of business altogether – one such man being renowned tobacco lord John Glassford, who died in 1783 with debts close to £100,000. However,

Trade and Industry

Glasgow had now enjoyed nearly a century of commercial success and Glasgow merchants continued to invest heavily in a wide range of activities including land, shipping and industry.

The manufacture of linen, lawns, cambrics and similar articles began in about 1725, and continued for some time to be the staple trade of the city and neighbourhood. But it was cotton that would bring renewed prosperity to Glasgow. The number of cotton mills within a radius of 25 miles of Glasgow rose from 19 to 134 between 1787 and 1834. Mill owners faced the considerably problem of finding an adequate labour supply. They met this need by using pauper children. Children comprised a remarkable 84 per cent of the employees in Renfrewshire's forty-one cotton mills in 1809, and 36 per cent of the workforce in Glasgow's cotton mills in 1833. The children were taken at the age of 6 or 7 from charity houses on long indentures, and virtually imprisoned in barrack-like accommodation. They were paid not much more than subsistence wages. To escape was to risk imprisonment, fines or beatings, as well as an extension of the indenture by twice the number of days the culprit was absent. Yet absconding was commonplace, not only among young millworkers, but also from the ranks of apprentices in occupations such as nail-making and calico-printing. Many sought a life in the army or abroad.

Mill owners also encouraged migrants from rural Scotland and from Ireland. They were favoured by employers because they would work for less wages than Lowland workers. The migrants included women and children, to the extent that in the early nineteenth century at least half of the workforce in the cotton mills and textile factories of Glasgow and Paisley were first-generation Irish migrants and their descendants.

Writing for the *Statistical Account, 1791–99*, the Revd John Burns noted the social change brought about by the cotton industry in Glasgow and the surrounding area:

> In the year 1784, a cotton mill was built at North Woodside in this parish, by Mr. William Gillespie, which give employment

Tobacco Lord from Robert Renwick, History of Glasgow.

to about 400 persons, men, women and children. This, with the people engaged in the bleachfield, and otherwise, has made Woodside a considerable village, while it has become the seat of plenty and comfort, the happy consequence of industry and manufactures.

Trade and Industry

The flourishing cotton industry also stimulated the development of related industries such as bleaching, dyeing and fabric printing. Robert Forsyth, observing Glasgow in 1805, commented:

> The cotton manufacture . . . together with the various arts dependent upon it, is now become the stable of the west of Scotland, and is here carried on to a greater extent than in any town in Britain, except Manchester . . . Neither is the trade confined to the workmen in the city: the manufacturers of Glasgow employ several thousand weavers who live in the district of the country around it, and even to the distance of thirty or forty miles. . . . This manufacture is not only important of itself, but is productive of work to many thousands of bleachers, tambourers, calico-printers, &c. many of whom being women and children, whose work was formerly unproductive, renders it of still more general interest. . . .
>
> When, in addition to these statements, the number of parties employed as operatives at other trades or occupations is taken into consideration, the conclusion will readily be arrived at that at least four-fifths of the population of the city of Glasgow and suburbs consist of the working classes and their families. This might also be inferred from the simple fact that only about 11,000 names are thought worthy of a place in the Glasgow Post-office Directory, and of these many are entered twice, first as members of firms, or copartneries, and secondly as private residents.

The eventual decline of the cotton industry was due in part to the development of more profitable industries – chemical works, calico-printing, distilling and potteries – but above all the iron trades. It was the steam engine that made modern Glasgow, enabling it at last to exploit the enormous coalfields of Lanarkshire and the cheap labour from Ireland and the Scottish Highlands. Iron founding had been introduced into Scotland in 1680, but the native ironstone was not employed until 1759, when the Carron Company erected iron furnaces and foundries near Falkirk. By the time these were connected by canal with the Clyde, a waterway had been made from Glasgow to the Monkland region, a few miles away, where great furnaces were set up at the pitheads. Iron foundries and engine works sprang up in Glasgow at the beginning of the nineteenth century, and with the application of Neilson's hot-blast to furnaces in 1829 production rapidly increased.

In the 1830s and 1840 the St Rollox Chemical Works in Springburn were the largest chemical works in the world with its 455ft chimney stack, at the time the tallest in Europe. By the 1850s St Rollox was churning out 60 tons of soap a week as well as various industrial alkalis. According to James Dawson Burn, in *Commercial Enterprise and Social Progress, or, Gleanings in London, Sheffield, Glasgow and Dublin* (1858):

> The most extraordinary part of the work is that in which the sulphuric acid is made . . . we pass between two mountains of sulphur, each of 5000 tons. We then enter a devil's den with an immense row of glowing furnaces . . . half roasted and our lungs struggling with the atmosphere, loaded with sulphuric gas . . . men moving about like spirits in the fitful glare of the fiery furnace.

Glasgow's status as a great trading port ensured it had a pool of skilled artisans including blacksmiths, wrights, carpenters and clockmakers who could put their expertise to good use in the new factories and shipbuilding yards. James Dawson Burn, in his *Commercial Enterprise and Social Progress, or, Gleanings in London, Sheffield, Glasgow and Dublin* (1858), noted that Glasgow was divided into several distinct regions characterised by the occupation of its inhabitants:

> The districts in which the labouring classes, tradesmen, and artisans reside, cover a large part of the city and suburbs. For

Trade and Industry

some years the Cowcaddens has been the seat of a numerous class of tradesmen and unskilled labourers. The same may be said of St. Rollox. The suburban district of Anderston, is full of a hardy, and an industrious race of mechanics, many thousands of whom are employed in the wood and iron shipbuilding yards. As we said before, the banks of the river for miles is one continued scene of human industry. The emporium of cotton lies on the south eastern quarter of the town in Bridgeton, and the Calton, where a vast number of people are employed, either in this branch of business or in others, depending upon it. Plutcheson, Gorbals, and Laurieston, are also filled with large industrial populations. During the last ten years, the iron trade in its various branches has furnished a rapidly increasing market for labour. In that short period of time, foundries, machine shops, engine makers, and boilermakers' establishments, have sprung into existence round the whole of the suburbs.

Very little shipbuilding was carried out until the late eighteenth century with most of the seagoing vessels sailing from the Firth of Clyde being built in America. After the American War of Independence a growing number of sailing ships were built at Greenock and Port Glasgow. By the beginning of the nineteenth century the deepening of the river by the Clyde Navigation Trust made it possible for ocean-going ships to reach right into the centre of the city.

The final impetus that started the Clyde on the road to becoming a world-famous centre for shipbuilding was the application of steam engines to sailing vessels. In 1812 self-taught engineer Henry Bell from Torphichen, West Lothian, built the *Comet*, the world's first successful passenger steamship, which sailed between Glasgow and Greenock and ushered in the rise of the Clyde's shipbuilding industry. Robert Gillespie recorded, in *Glasgow and the Clyde* (1876), how shipbuilding was contributing to the development of the city:

The city is undoubtedly spreading fastest to the west along the course of the river – a circumstance to be attributed to the extraordinary prosperity of the shipbuilding trade. Partick on the north and Govan on the south, which only a few years ago were separated from Glasgow by an interval of from one to two miles, have already been touched by the process of extension and passed. Whiteinch and Partick are all but conterminous, and from the former it is but a step to Dalmuir. Indeed the bridging of the intervening space has already been begun, by the erection of a large shipbuilding yard, with workmen's houses lining the road. The same process is going on upon the south bank below Govan. Shipbuilding establishments are travelling fast downwards, driven from their old locations by successive additions to the harbour space. But although down the Clyde is the main line of extension, north, south, and east the city is moving ever onwards and enlarging her boundaries.

Portrait of Henry Bell, *before 1830, artist unknown.*

The Clyde's annual shipbuilding output rose from 20,000 tons in 1850 to nearly 500,000 by 1900 and peaked at nearly 800,000 tons just before the First World War. Fitting out these vast ocean liners, or equipping their military and mercantile counterparts, employed an estimated 100,000 artisans from every imaginable trade.

The great engineering works, shipbuilding enterprises and railway companies all consumed vast amounts of coal. Coal mining

Trade and Industry

had been established in the Clyde valley by the seventeenth century, and in the eighteenth the use of coal in the local iron, pottery and glass manufacturing increased demand and production. The opening of the Monkland Canal in 1792 facilitated the transport of coal from the Lanarkshire coalfields to Glasgow reducing prices in the growing town.

There were also coalfields within the expanding boundaries of Glasgow. The most important centres of mining were in the east of the city around Tollcross, Shettleston and Mount Vernon, and the largest collieries, employing between 500 and 1,000 miners each, included Govan, Kenmuirhill, Viewpark and Bargeddie. There were also large mines immediately to the south in Rutherglen, Uddingston, Cambuslang, Bothwell and Giffnock, notable examples being Farme, Blantyreferme and Thornliebank.

Life and conditions down the mines were tough. The report by Thomas Tancred to the Children's Employment Commission on the West of Scotland District, which was published in 1842, included interviews with colliers such as James Scott, aged 18. He had spent some of his formative years at the House of Refuge until his brother found employment at Mr Dixon's pits at Brigend near Gorbals.

> When his brother had picked out the coal at the face of the seam, his work was to split it and shovel it into 'hutches', which are small carts made of iron in which boys draw the coal to the bottom of the shaft; no horses being employed in these pits. The seam of coal in which he worked was not quite five feet thick; he could stand upright in it then, but not now. The pit was wrought night and day, and with the two sets of boys had about 200 altogether. He had to take his turn a fortnight at a time in the 'day shift', and the same in the night one. The engine starts to draw up the coal about six o'clock morning, and the boys generally go down about half past four, 'by stairs', not by the engine. There were 50 steps to go down. He left work about six in the evening. He took down bread and

milk or coffee, as much as would serve till night, and had no regular hours for meals, but just eat them when he was waiting at the bottom of the shaft till it was his turn to have his coals hoisted up.

As with the mills, children were employed in large numbers down the pit and soon displayed the physical consequences of such hard work. A report *On the Diseases, Conditions, and Habits of the Collier Population of East Lothian* by S. Scott Alison (1842) found that 'Many of the infants in a collier community are thin, skinny, and wasted, and indicate by their contracted features and sickly dirty-white, or faint-yellowish aspect, their early participation in a deteriorated physical condition.'

The report found that this inferiority was caused by a variety of causes, such as:

unwholesome milk, the product of a mother the victim of disease or of intemperate habits; the irregular and insufficient supply of milk, in consequence of the absence of the mother, who is engaged in the colliery; the indiscriminate and premature use of coarse and irritating food, which frequently induces relaxation of the bowels, and the manifold ailments which collier people group under the title of 'bowel hive'; the too long continued exclusive use of the mother's milk, which not infrequently forms the chief sustenance of the infant for the first eighteen months or two years of its existence – a course too frequently pursued in order to save the pockets and the exertions of the parents; a filthy condition of the person; the presence of the alvine and urinary discharges upon the skin and clothes, which not only irritate the integuments and interfere with its functions, but which very frequently produce such an impure atmosphere around the little victim as must be very unfavourable to its health and vigour.

Life for women was also tough. The report found that:

> Several of them are distorted in the spine and pelvis, and suffer considerable difficulty in consequence at the period of parturition; but I am inclined to think, where this has not arisen from direct violence, that it has been induced by general debility and bad habit of body, induced in infancy or childhood. Many women at this age are found to suffer from the effects of violence. The violence has generally proceeded from contusions from collision with wagons, from the fall of stones and coals; and the effects of this violence are lameness, imperfection in motions of the limbs, hands, and feet, abortion and premature parturition.

As for the colliers, the report concluded that 'It was rare to find a perfectly healthy collier after thirty and the decline in health after this age was rapid. By the fiftieth year comparatively few survive.'

With the onset of the Depression after the First World War coal mining stagnated and by 1934 the number of mines in and around Glasgow had fallen by two-thirds. Garscube Colliery in Maryhill had however been re-opened and an important new development on the eastern edge of the city at Stepps, Cardowan Colliery, had commenced production of coking coal for Messrs Nimmo & Dunlop in 1929. Nevertheless, the overall decline continued and by nationalisation in 1947 only Garscube, Cardowan, Blantyreferme, Bardykes and Coatspark had survived. The National Coal Board developed a temporary drift mine at Greenlees near Cambuslang in 1948, but this worked for only ten years. Thereafter, no new mines were sunk in the city.

KEY SOURCES
Glasgow City Archives hold records from over 300 businesses that were based in or around Glasgow. These range from large companies

Women operating machinery at J. & P. Coats Ltd. (Glasgow University Archives)

that employed huge numbers of workers, to small local businesses. Business records can include company minutes, financial records, annual reports, brochures and personnel records. Of most interest to family historians are personnel records, such as wage books, apprenticeship registers, staff photographs and accident books. However, personnel records have not always survived, which means tracing ancestors using this source can be difficult.

The City Archives hold the records of the Merchants House and the Trades House of Glasgow, the fifteen individual craft incorporations within the city, as well as the records of crafts from surrounding areas. These include:

Trade and Industry

Records of the Merchants House and the Trades House of Glasgow		
Title	Date	Reference
Merchants House of Glasgow	1558–1975	T-MH
Trades House of Glasgow	1597–1975	T-TH1
Hammermen of Glasgow	1616–1934	T-TH2
Tailors of Glasgow	1504–1974	T-TH3
Cordiners of Glasgow	1550–1961	T-TH4
Weavers of Glasgow	1504–1974	T-TH5
Maltmen of Glasgow	1615–1977	T-TH6
Bakers of Glasgow	1574–1961	T-TH7
Skinners of Glasgow	13th c.–1976	T-TH8
Wrights of Glasgow (see Masons up to 1600)	1650–1977	T-TH9
Coopers of Glasgow	15th c.–1910	T-TH10
Fleshers of Glasgow	1576–1968	T-TH11
Masons of Glasgow (including Wrights until 1600)	14th c.–1976	T-TH12
Gardiners of Glasgow	1626–1986	T-TH13
Barbers of Glasgow (including Surgeons to 1722)	1656–1962	T-TH14
Bonnet-makers and Dyers of Glasgow	13th c.–1957	T-TH15
Framework Knitters and Stocking Makers of Glasgow	1756–1904	T-TH16
Weavers of Anderston	1754–1985	T-TH2 & TD1615
Hammermen of Calton	1789–1854	TD105
Weavers of Govan	1756–1963	TD1740
Weavers of Rutherglen	1641–1871	RU9/1

Council Registers of Licences

Glasgow City Archives holds the records of those licensed or registered by the city council to practise a particular trade. Glasgow Corporation was empowered during the nineteenth century to issue these licenses or registrations. These included retailers and moneylenders as well as those who provided public transport.

Licensed Occupations		
Title	Dates	Reference
Brokers	1935–52	E7/9/1-3
Chimney Sweeps	1852–62	B8/17
	1934–52	E7/16/1-3
Domestic Servants, Keepers of	1938–52	E7/20/1
Drivers of Hackney Carriages	1939–52	E7/23/1-5
Fireworks, retailers of	1930–52	E7/14/1-2
Metal Refiners	1914–52	E7/19/1
Moneylenders	1927–51	B8/21
Pawnbrokers	1844–63	B8/22
Pedlars under the Act of 1871	1939–65	E7/11/1-3
Porters	1798, 1847–71	B8/18/1-2
	1921–52	E7/10/1
Porters, City and Harbour	1834–68	B8/19
Porters, Harbour	1834–68	B8/20
Publicans (Ale)	1779–1804, 1815–24	B8/4
Publicans (Ale and Spirits)	1824–98	B8/6
Publicans (Applicants)	1898–1968	B8/7
Publicans (Govan Burgh)	1904–12	B8/16/1
Publicans (Partick Burgh)	1902–12	B8/16/2
Publicans (Pollokshaws Burgh)	1904–12	B8/16/3
Publicans (Spirits)	1818–24	B8/5
Street Traders	1949 only	E7/12/1
Street Trading	1949 only	E7/13/1
Window Cleaners	1937–52	E7/17/1-4
Window Cleaners	1931–53	E7/18/1-2

Trade and Industry

The Register of Chimney Sweeps licensed by the Burgh of Glasgow, 1852–62 is available online at http://www.glasgowfamilyhistory.org.uk/ExploreRecords/Documents/Chimney%20Sweeps.pdf.

The **Scottish Business Archive at Glasgow University** covers almost all types of business and industrial activity in Scotland and the United Kingdom with over 400 collections from banking, confectioners and distillers to retail, solicitors and undertakers. Its holdings are particularly strong in relation to industrial concerns in the west of Scotland such as shipbuilding, railway locomotive manufacture, textiles and mining. They contain a wide variety of records including minute books, financial ledgers, legal documents, marketing material, production papers, staff records and photographs, providing invaluable insights into all areas of business activity.

Directories

The first Glasgow directory was published in 1783 by John Tait. It consisted of 103 pages and contained the names of over 1,700 persons. In his preface Tait states that 'the publisher did make an actual survey of a great number of houses, shops, warehouses, etc [but] many had scruples of giving information'. The next directory was published by Nathaniel Jones in 1787 as a *Directory, or Useful Pocket Companion* with 1,552 names. He also produced issues for 1789 and 1792. From 1799 it became an annual publication and by 1825 the number listed had risen to over 6,000. In 1828 it became the *Glasgow Post Office Directory* and included merchants, traders, manufacturers and principal inhabitants. The series continued to appear for well over 130 years recording a street by street expansion of the city.

The following directories are available to view online at the National Library of Scotland (NLS) website at http://www.nls.uk/family-history/directories/post-office/index.cfm?place=Glasgow:

- **1783–4**: John Tait's 'directory for the City of Glasgow ... also for the towns of Paisley, Greenock, Port-Glasgow, and Kilmarnock, from the 15th May, 1783, to the 15th May 1784, etc.'.

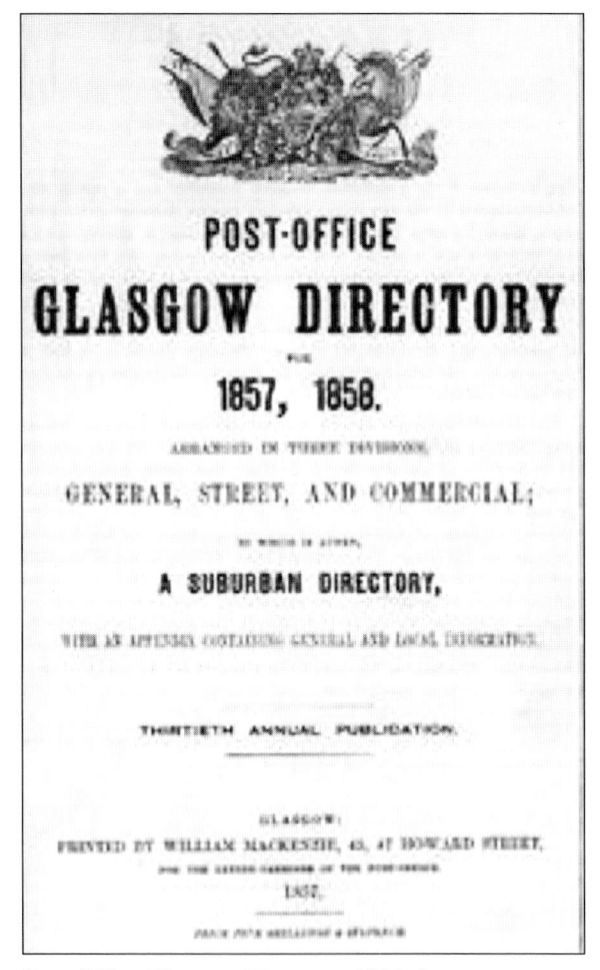

Post Office Glasgow Directory, 1857–8.

- **1787**: Reprint of Jones's *Directory, or Useful Pocket Companion*.
- **1789**: Jones's *Directory, or Useful Pocket Companion*.
- **1790–1**: Jones's *Directory, or Useful Pocket Companion*.
- **1799–1912 (excluding 1802, 1808 and 1816)**: *Glasgow Post Office Directory*.

Trade and Industry

The **Mitchell Library** has the following directories for Glasgow:

- **1921–74**, for most years: *Kelly's Directory Glasgow*.
- **1906–28**, for most years: *Glasgow Trades Directory*.
- **1902–67**, intermittent coverage: *Glasgow and Lanark Trades Directory*.
- **1902–66**, intermittent coverage: *Glasgow and West of Scotland Trades Directory*.
- **1889 to date**, coverage for most years for each decade: *Phone Books* for Glasgow.
- **1929 to date**, coverage for most years for each decade: *Yellow Pages* for Glasgow.

The *Phone Books* and *Yellow Pages* for Glasgow list the names, addresses and phone numbers of residential and business customers respectively.

Chapter 8

TRANSPORT

The rapid expansion of the Glasgow economy in the second half of the eighteenth century meant that large quantities of goods had to be moved quickly around the country. Unfortunately, the roads of Scotland were pretty basic, dry and dusty in summer, wet and boggy in winter. The problem was so bad in Glasgow that it was decided to make the River Clyde deep enough for ships rather than rely on goods being carried by road to Port Glasgow.

Attempts were, nevertheless, made to improve the road system. An Act in 1669 made it the job of every parish to maintain roads and all parishioners were obliged to work on their upkeep. This proved unpopular and in 1750 the Turnpike Act was passed, allowing roads to be built privately and the owners to charge for their use. These improvements led to an increase in the number of road users and this was especially true for horse-drawn coaches.

Passenger travel by stagecoach had developed considerably in the second half of the eighteenth century. The first Glasgow–Greenock coach began to run in 1763, taking 9 hours to complete the journey. The first Glasgow–Aberdeen coach, taking six days, ran in 1780 and the following year the first Glasgow–Carlisle diligence, connecting there with the coach for London, began to operate. It was claimed that in good conditions the Glasgow–London journey could take four days and by 1789 this had been reduced to 66 hours. In 1819 eight public coaches with four horses, and seven with two horses, left and returned to Glasgow daily: one to London, five to Edinburgh, three to Paisley, two to Greenock and one each to Perth, Ayr, Hamilton and Kilmarnock.

Eighteenth- and early nineteenth-century newspapers carry advertisements for coach services. The following comes from the *Caledonian Mercury*, 2 April 1752:

> The GLASGOW STAGE COACH sets out on Monday next the 6th current at Six o'clock in the Morning, through in one Day. Tickets to be had at Mr. Cockayne's New Inn, Glasgow. The MUSSELBURUGH STAGE COACH to set out on Monday next at Ten o'clock before Noon, and continues to every Day, and returns from Musselburgh at Four Afternoon. And upon the 17th current a COACH to set out for London from John Paxton's at the Foot of the Cannongate; where Coaches, Chariots, Chaises, and Landaus may be had, at any Time, to any part of Britain.

CANALS

In spite of the Turnpike Acts, roads connecting Glasgow with the outside world remained pretty primitive throughout the eighteenth century. A canal linking the Clyde with the Forth seemed an obvious way to improve communications with the city. When the **Forth and Clyde Canal**, also known as the **Great Canal**, opened in 1790, it was the biggest single venture undertaken in Scotland up to that time and a source of great national pride. It provided vital trade and transport links, with over 3 million tonnes of goods and 200,000 passengers being transported each year by the mid-1800s. A collateral cut extended the canal nearer the city where a large set of basins and wharves were constructed and christened Port Dundas. Factories of all sorts sprang up, including chemical works, dye-works, foundries, machine shops, potteries and distilleries.

The Forth and Clyde Canal began to go into decline as the seagoing vessels were built on a larger scale and could no longer pass through. The railway age further impaired the success of the canal and it was taken over by the Caledonian Railway Company in 1867. It was finally closed in the 1960s, although it had been largely

View of the Glasgow & Monkland Canal, 1824–6. (Glasgow University Archives)

stagnant for decades. The M8 motorway in the eastern approaches to Glasgow took over some of the alignment of the canal.

Glasgow's progress as an industrial city required vast quantities of cheap coal. The opening of the **Monkland Canal** in 1792 facilitated the transport of coal from the Lanarkshire coalfields to Glasgow and reduced coal prices in the city. The Monkland Canal was bought in 1846 by the Forth and Clyde Canal company (taken over by the Caledonian Railway in 1867). The Monkland Canal was closed to commercial traffic in 1935 and was abandoned in 1950.

The **Glasgow, Paisley and Ardrossan Canal**, later known as the **Glasgow, Paisley and Johnstone Canal**, was a canal in the west of Scotland, running between the booming industrial towns of Glasgow, Paisley and Johnstone; it was completed in 1811. Despite the name, the canal was never continued to Ardrossan, the termini being Port Eglinton in Glasgow and Thorn Brae in Johnstone. Shareholders included William Dixon of Govan who wished to export coal from his Govan colliery. The canal continued to compete with the railways for many decades, but in 1869, was purchased by the Glasgow & South Western Railway Company and was closed in

1881. Much of the route was used to construct the Paisley Canal railway line.

The **Edinburgh and Glasgow Union Canal** was built as an uninterrupted 'contour canal' connected to the Forth and Clyde Canal by a flight of eleven locks at Camelon (Falkirk). This provided a direct inland connection between Glasgow and Edinburgh, as well as the east and west coasts. In addition to coal, the canals carried passengers between the cities. Once again mounting competition from rail and coach led to major, early decline. After a takeover by the Forth and Clyde Canal Company fell through, its assets were vested in the Edinburgh and Glasgow Railway Company in 1849. In 1921 the eastern terminus was curtailed and the western end followed suit in 1933 when commercial traffic ceased. The Falkirk lock flight was filled in during the 1930s and at places like Westerhailes and Broxburn the canal was culverted to make way for new roads to be built. The Union Canal was formally closed to navigation in August 1965.

Canal Records
NRS holds the records of canals in a number of different series. These include the following:

- **The Edinburgh and Glasgow Union Canal**: the NRS holds the main series of minutes of the Committee of Subscribers, 1813–1922 (Ref. BR/EGU/1/1-9).
- **Forth and Clyde Canal**: the minutes of the Forth and Clyde Canal date from 1767 and are the earliest and fullest set of canal company minute books in the NRS. The surviving minutes, 1767–1850 are now amalgamated under Ref. BR/FCN/1/1-97.
- **The Glasgow Paisley and Johnstone Canal**: the NRS holds the company minute books, 1815–40 and records relating to undertakings, reports, rates etc. (Ref. BR/GPA). An earlier minute book, 1805–17, is among the Court of Session papers (Ref. CS96/2002).

- **The Monkland Canal**: records of the Monkland Canal are held by the NRS but papers relating to the Monkland Canal Navigation, 1837–46 are also found in the Monkland & Kirkintilloch Railway Archive held by the Glasgow University Library.

The records of the **Clyde Navigation Trust** are held by Glasgow City Archives and are a wonderful source of information about Glasgow's trading history and the creation of the Clyde as an international waterway. The records include:

- Minutes, the main records of the trust from 1801.
- Reports and papers, recording all aspects of the Clyde and Clyde Navigation, 1755–1958, including reports from the country's leading engineers, John Smeaton, John Golborne, Thomas Telford and others.
- Accounts and statistics, detailing the rise of Glasgow as a world trading centre.
- Report books, these record ships entering and leaving the Clyde (both Glasgow and Greenock), 1819–1968, but do not include passengers' names.
- *Clyde Bill of Entry*, local newspaper, listing arrivals and departures of ships for the Clyde, with details of cargo etc., 1841–87.
- Photographs, thousands of photographs, including construction of works, buildings, cranes and equipment, ships and views of the Clyde. Only a few of these are on the Virtual Mitchell.
- Maps and plans, including general plans of the river and riparian lands, plans of bridges, weirs, canals, railways, lighthouses and the harbour.

Records of the Lord Advocate's Department reveal a small number of canal workers who found themselves on the wrong side of the law (NRS Ref. AD14/19-22). The Forth and Clyde Canal records include documents relating to uniforms issued to staff, holidays etc., 1904–9 (NRS Ref. BR/FCN/4/10).

RAILWAYS

The development of the railways brought about a second Industrial Revolution in Scotland. Before the growth of rail travel people moved about at much the same pace as they had done for a thousand years. The railway age reached Glasgow in 1831 when the **Glasgow & Garnkirk Railway** opened. Although the line carried passengers, it was primarily designed for the movement of goods and played an important role in reducing the cost of coal in the city.

The next two lines to be opened were of greater importance. In August 1840 the **Glasgow & Ayrshire Railway** began operations between Bridge Street station (on the south bank of the Clyde, near the Jamaica Bridge) and Ayr, via Paisley, Kilwinning and Irvine. It was the opening of this line that enabled passengers from Glasgow to reach London in the amazing time of 24 hours, by taking a train to Ardrossan on the Firth of Clyde, then a steamer to Liverpool and from there travelling by train to London. The **Glasgow & Greenock line** was authorised at the same time as the Ayrshire (1837) and was opened in June 1841.

The fourth Glasgow railway, the **Edinburgh & Glasgow**, was the first trunk line in Scotland when it opened in February 1842. Its Glasgow terminus, **Queen's Street station**, was located at the north-west corner of George Square. The line was completed to Glasgow and Edinburgh, along with line to Castlecary, Stirlingshire in 1848 where it joined the Scottish Central Railway. The line to Glasgow utilised the earlier railways Glasgow, Garnkirk & Coatbridge and the Wishaw & Coltness, which it purchased in 1846 and 1849 respectively and ran into Queen Street station.

The railways caused a social revolution. The speed of travel increased and the agricultural areas outside Glasgow had a cheap and easy means of getting their produce to the city. Within a few years of the first passengers services having been established, people were looking back in wonder at the changes that had taken place

St Enoch station, Glasgow, Valentine's Series postcard of 1911.

since the age of the stagecoach. The following entry was published in the *Leeds Intelligencer*, 23 May 1846:

> GLASGOW STATE COACH v RAILWAYS – The first stage coach from Edinburgh to Glasgow was established, by contract, between the Glasgow magistrates and William Hume, a merchant of Edinburgh, in the year 1678. He was to have 'in readinesses and sufficient strong coach to run betwixt Edinbro' and Glasgow; to run by six able horses, to leave Edinbro' on Monday and returns again (God willing) on Saturday night. The burgesses of Glasgow always to have a preference to the coach'. Probably at this time the passengers weekly, to and from Glasgow per coach, would number about twenty-four. In one day alone last week, the passengers by the Edinburgh and Glasgow Railway numbered 2000. So much for the march of improvement.

Transport

Gangs of navvies were recruited from the canal and railway construction industry in England. It took a year on the railway to make a labourer into a navvy who could work a full day shifting 'muck', as the heavy clay was called. Many were extended families of workmen from different parts of Ireland and some were from Liverpool and Scotland. They were paid a piece-work rate, which was essentially earning according to the amount of muck they could shift, the quantity being assessed by overseers who measured the loads in wheelbarrows. An experienced navvy could shift about 20 tons of clay in a 12-hour day using a pick and shovel. He could put away 2lb of beef per day washed down with a dozen quarts of beer. Little wonder that their life expectancy was short. Navvies followed the work; few had settled wives with them, but they formed makeshift family groupings with the women who joined them in the encampments and shanty dwellings which grew up around the line of the railway.

The railway network integrated the country as never before, as travel was now possible for people with little leisure and no private transport. For the fortunate, railways made it possible to live at a distance from the place of employment, and suburbs arose around the cities, providing more work for architects, masons, builders, carpenters and slaters, plumbers and painters. Industrial costs were dramatically lowered and profits soared accordingly. Production of coal and iron (and steel) was in greatly increased demand and new jobs at all levels were provided – labourers to lay the tracks and civil engineers to plan them; mechanical engineers to design locomotives; labourers to smelt the iron ore; platers and riveters to build them; drivers and firemen to crew the engines; and signalmen and surfacemen to see to the safe scheduled running of the trains.

By the 1860s the general outline of the Scottish rail network was virtually complete. In 1865 the **North British Railway** (the largest Scottish railway) merged with the Edinburgh and Glasgow. At the grouping of the railways in 1923, the North British Railway was the largest railway company in Scotland, and the fifth largest in the United Kingdom.

The **Caledonian Railway** was formed in the early nineteenth century with the objective of creating a link between English railways and Glasgow. It progressively extended its network soon reaching Edinburgh and Aberdeen, with a dense network of branch lines in the area surrounding Glasgow. Access to Glasgow was orginally by traversing the early Garnkirk line to Townhead, but larger terminal facilities were soon gained at Bridge Street in 1849 and the Clyde was crossed to the site of the present **Central station** thirty years later. In 1885 the Central Station Hotel was opened on the corner of Gordon and Hope Streets; with nearly 400 bedrooms it easily surpassed the rival establishments at St Enoch station. Like the North British Railway, the Caledonian had its own underground line running north and south under the city. Services to and from Glasgow and the north used **Buchanan Street** terminus, which closed in 1966.

The **Glasgow & South Western Railway** was formed by the amalgamation of the Glasgow, Dumfries & Carlisle and the Glasgow Kilmarnock & Ayr Railways, and became best known for its services from Glasgow to the Clyde coast and to Stranraer which passed through Kilmarnock and Dumfries to Carlisle. Its Glasgow terminus was **St Enoch**, which closed in 1966. It later formed an alliance with the English Midland Railway and ran express passenger trains from Glasgow to London with that company, in competition with the Caledonian Railway and its English partner, who had an easier route.

The **Railways Act**, also known as the **Grouping Act**, which came into operation in 1923, created the 'Big Four' railway companies in an attempt to stem the losses being made by many of the country's 120 railway companies and to move the railways away from internal competition. The Caledonian Railway and the Glasgow & South Western Railway were absorbed into the **London, Midland & Scottish Railway** and the North British Railway into the **London & Northern Eastern Railway**, which operated until nationalisation on 1 January 1948 and the creation of British Railways.

A 'double-headed' North British Railway express climbing Cowlairs Bank, c. 1900. (Photograph by Dr Tice F. Budden)

Railway engines have been described as Glasgow's second heavy industry (shipbuilding being the first) and it was concentrated almost entirely at the Hyde Park and Atlas works in Springburn. An amalgamation in 1903 produced the **North British Locomotive Company**, which was the largest in Europe with 60 acres of workshops and over 8,000 employees. Most production was for export, India taking over 11,000 steam and diesel engines, many of which have outlasted the works that produced them.

Railway Records

After the North British Locomotive Company went into liquidation in 1962, the photographic records were deposited in the Mitchell Library. This became the North British Locomotive Collection, consisting of about 9,000 glass negatives and approximately 6,500 photographic prints.

Glasgow University Archives holds papers relating to the **North British Locomotive Company** within the Andrew Barclay Archive (Ref. GD 329) and the North British Locomotive Co. Ltd

Archive (Ref. UGD 11). Records relating to the production of locomotives are held with GD 329, with the locomotive plans having the reference prefix RHP.

Glasgow University Archives also holds records of the **Glasgow & South Western Railway Company** (1850–1923) which includes papers regarding the Ardrossan Railway (Refs GB 248 UGB 008/7 and UGB 8/38). It also holds records of the **Edinburgh & Glasgow Railway Company** (1838–65) which includes papers relating to the Forth of Clyde Navigation (Ref. GB 248 UGB/008/06); papers of the Monkland & Kirkintilloch Railway (1824–48) which includes papers relating to the Monkland Canal Navigation (Ref. GB 248 UGD/008/ 2).

The NRS holds the largest written and pictorial archive of Scottish railway history. The bulk of the collection is made up of the records formerly held by the British Transport Records Historical Records Department in Edinburgh and passed to the NRS by the terms of the Transport Act 1968 (section 144) (NRS Ref. BR).

The NRS also holds collections of more recent records deposited by the British Railways Board, British Railways (Scottish Region), British Rail Board (Residuary), Scotrail, Railtrack Scotland and Network Rail. The company records contain minutes and reports, letter books, deeds and agreements, circulars, locomotive and rolling stock records, civil engineers records, station traffic books, accident reports and staff records. In addition, the NRS has an important collection of specialised books and periodicals on transport subjects, mostly inherited from the old railway companies and dating back to the 1840s, as well as timetables, publicity material and a large series of engineering and architectural drawings.

The **Caledonian Railway Association** was established in 1983 to promote the study, acquisition and preservation of information, documents, illustrations and artefacts relating to the Caledonian Railway and its successor companies. These records are stored at Glasgow University Archives and include staff records, 1890–1939 and drawings and plans of locomotives, rolling stock, railway lines, stations and property.

Opening of the Glasgow & Garnkirk Railway, 1831. This lithograph was one of a series made by the pioneering photographer and artist David Octavius Hill, printed by W. Day of London in 1832 and sold by Tilt and Ackermann.

Ancestry.com has a database UK, Railway Employment Records, 1833–1956 which includes indexed images of employment-related records from a number of historic railway companies in England, Scotland and Wales. This can be searched online at http://search.ancestry.co.uk/.

Underground and Tramways

Glasgow's underground railway system is the only one in Scotland, and the third oldest in the world after London and Budapest. In August 1890, the Glasgow District Subway Co. was given authority to build a 6.5-mile long route under the streets of Glasgow. The underground was opened on 14 December 1896, but a collision that day meant that the network did not start operating until 21 January 1897.

Tracing Your Glasgow Ancestors

The trains were originally moved by gripping a continuous moving cable, which was moved by a coal-fired boiler in Scotland Street on the south side of Glasgow. The network has fifteen stations, seven south of the River Clyde and eight to the north. Buchanan Street, St Enoch and Partick stations provide interchanges with the mainline railways. The Glasgow Corporation was running the largest tram network in Britain when it took over the company in 1923. In 1935 the decision was taken to electrify the railway to reduce operating costs. In 1973 the Greater Glasgow Passenger Transport Executive took over control of the Glasgow underground.

Glasgow Corporation Tramways formerly operated one of the largest urban tramway systems in Europe. Over 1,000 municipally owned trams served the city with over 100 route miles (160 route kilometres) by 1922. The system closed in 1962 and was the last city tramway in Great Britain (prior to the construction of new systems in the 1990s).

Glasgow's tramlines had a highly unusual track gauge of 4ft 7¾in (1,416mm). This was to permit 4ft 8½in (1,435mm) standard gauge railway wagons to be operated over parts of the tram system (particularly in the Govan area) using their wheel flanges running in the slots of the tram tracks. This allowed the railway wagons to be drawn along tramway streets to access some shipyards. The shipyards provided their own small electric locomotives, running on the tramway power, to pull these wagons, principally loaded with steel for shipbuilding, from local railway freight yards.

The records of the **Glasgow Corporation Transport Department** are held at Glasgow City Archives (Ref. D-TR). Unfortunately, these do not include many employment records but they do hold the superannuation registers for the department (Ref. D-TR Superann). There is restricted access to these records as they contain personal, financial information. The information is no longer protected if the individual has passed away and a fully transcribed entry can be sent to a searcher once staff have seen a copy of the employee's death certificate.

If you have found an ancestor who worked for the council, there are various sources that you can use to research their employment:

- Glasgow Corporation annual lists of mainly white-collar workers, 1899–1975.
- Glasgow Corporation Transport Department superannuation records, 1923–83.

Chapter 9

EDUCATION

SCHOOLS
Before the Reformation there were two kinds of school in Scotland. The first was the lecture school, where children were taught in the vernacular. The higher category of school was the grammar school, where pupils were taught Latin and the humanities generally. Most of the principal towns in Scotland boasted burgh or grammar schools which were under the control of the Church, and one of the most outstanding of these was in Glasgow. But with the rapid expansion of the town during the nineteenth century some 300 schools were established in Glasgow which included a large number of private or adventure schools, Church schools, charitable or free schools, run either directly by the parish churches or through some charitable institution, and above these about 40 Higher Grade Schools which sought to prepare the city's youth for the universities and professions.

However, in a city dominated by factories and mills, the authorities faced a major battle ensuring children old enough to work attended any school at all. According to Robert Somers, in Glasgow in 1857, under half the population aged between 5 and 10 was attending school at all:

> Every branch of skilled labour as well as our shops and warehouses, offer employment to little boys who can read and scrawl their names. For a still less educated class, there are the factories, the bleachfields, the tobacco-works and a host of minor manufactures. Making matches, stringing beads or

Education

bugles on ladies' dresses, and a hundred other trivial occupations, absorb the labour of multitudes of children of both sexes, irrespective almost of age and totally irrespective of their instruction.

By the end of the 1860s it was estimated that two out of every five Glasgow children still did not attend any school. This was brought to an end by the passing of the 1872 Education (Scotland) Act, which made education for all children under 13 compulsory and school boards were set up throughout Scotland to run this new education system. The Glasgow School Board was established in 1873 and its 15 members were chosen by popular vote from an electorate of over 100,000 including women (unlike the parliamentary ones of the time).

Glasgow Grammar School. (Glasgow University Library, Special Collections)

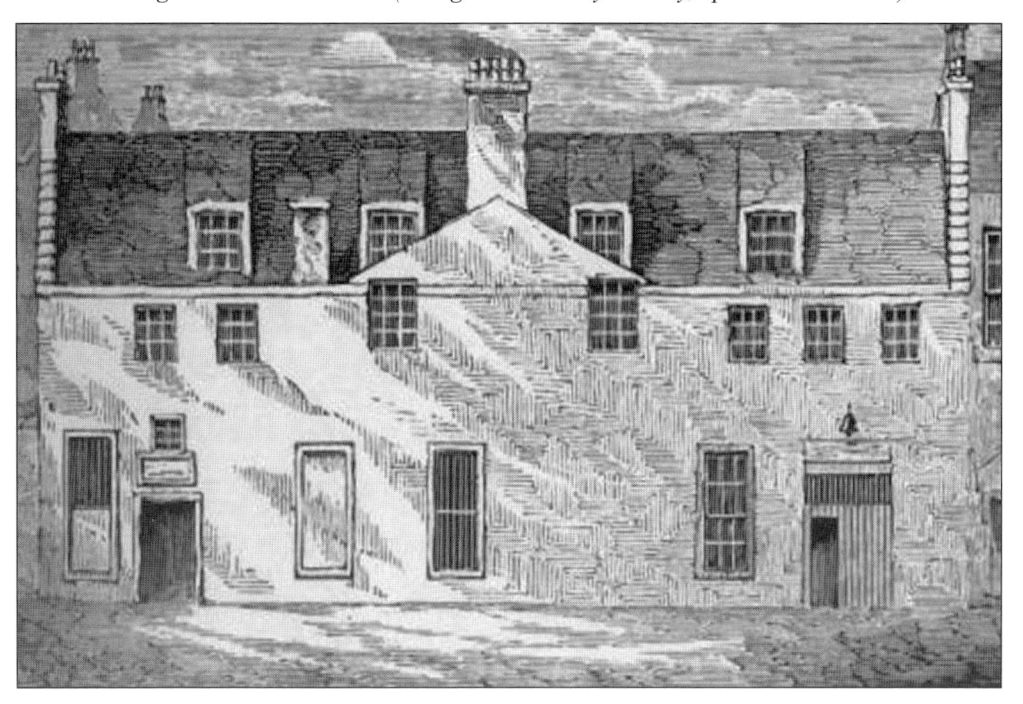

The Glasgow School Board had about 87,000 children in the city of school age but only about 200 schools capable of accommodating some 57,000 pupils. To meet this the board acquired 9 permanent day schools in Anderston, Bridgeton, Buchan Street, Dobbie's Loan, Finnieston, Hozier Street, Old Wynd, Rose Street and St Rollox, and opened temporary schools in various places until 30 schools with accommodation for 22,000 scholars could be instituted. By 1893 the board had established five secondary schools – **City School, John Street School, Kent Road School, Whitehill School** and **Woodside School** – in locations to cover the whole city. These were classified as Higher Grade Schools and to them were added the High School and Garnethill School (later the Glasgow High School for Girls). They were strategically placed to make sure that every child in the board area had the opportunity to continue in education beyond the age of 13. By 1908 the Glasgow School Board had a roll of some 80,000 pupils attending over 70 schools.

In the nineteenth century the rising middle class of the city's Roman Catholics began to look for a suitable education for their sons. **St Mungo's Academy** was founded by the Marist Brothers in 1858 at Garngad Hill to educate poor Catholic boys, largely Irish immigrants or their children. It sought to create a Catholic professional class by educating the boys to secondary level and preparing them for university studies. In this it had a good level of success, as well as providing a steady stream of boys wishing to pursue a career in the priesthood or other religious orders. **St Aloysius' College**, an independent Jesuit school in Glasgow, was founded in 1859 at Charlotte Green, in the East End of Glasgow. It was the centre of a large migrant Catholic community from Ireland and the Scottish Highlands.

There was a wide range of other schools financed by philanthropists, churches and charities. Some were aimed at specific groups. Some had very unusual criteria for admission. According to the *Ordnance Gazetteer of Scotland*:

Education

Alexander's charity, in Duke Street, affords a gratuitous education to children of the surname of Alexander or Anderson, children who have constantly resided for three years in High Church, St John's, or College parishes, or such children as the governors may select and appoint. The Logan and Johnston school, in Greenhead Street, was founded by the late William Logan and his wife, Jean Johnston, for the education, upbringing, and assistance in life of poor or destitute step-children or orphans of Scottish extraction, those bearing the names of Logan or Johnston to be preferred. One hundred and thirty girls receive instruction in the elementary branches of education, and also in knitting and sewing, and each of them receives lunch daily, and a suit of clothes, and two pairs of shoes and stockings yearly. The Maxwell and Hutcheson charitable trust was founded in 1877 under the will of Miss Ann Maxwell Graham of Williamwood, for the benefit of decayed gentlefolks of the names of Maxwell and Hutcheson, or their husbands, wives, or descendants, and also for the education of their children.

For centuries the only choice for the sons of the well-to-do was **Glasgow's Burgh** or **Grammar School**, which had been erected by 1460 in Grammar School Wynd, behind the west front of High Street opposite Blackfriars Church. It had become ruinous by 1600 and so a new building was erected in its place, with funds including 400 marks bequeathed to the University of Glasgow by 'Hary the porter of the College'. The school moved to George Street in the late 1780s and again, to John Street, in 1821. The Grammar School initially specialised in teaching Latin and Greek grammar, prose and composition. During the 1800s, the industrial growth of Glasgow created the need for a new type of education which would prepare the city's youth for entry to the universities and professions, and in response the High School in the 1830s radically enlarged its curriculum to include English, mathematics, geography, modern languages, physics and chemistry. In 1834 the Grammar School was renamed the **High School** and in 1872 it was transferred to the management of the Glasgow School Board. In 1878, the school moved into the former premises of the Glasgow Academy on Elmbank Street, when the latter moved to its new home in Kelvinbridge in the West End of the city. Former pupils included two prime ministers, Henry Campbell-Bannerman and Andrew Bonar Law.

The expansion of Glasgow's middle class meant that a series of independent schools were founded in Glasgow during the nineteenth century. **Glasgow Academy**, founded in 1845, is the oldest continuously fully independent school in the city. It aimed to meet the needs of the expanding western area of the city in which 'secular knowledge would be taught on evangelistic principles'. **Kelvinside Academy** in the Kelvinside area of the north of Glasgow, near the Glasgow Botanic Gardens, was founded in 1878, to meet the continuing expansion of Glasgow's West End as a high-class residential area. It faced strong competition from Glasgow Academy which moved into the area that same year.

Allan Glen's School was founded by the Allan Glen's Endowment Scholarship Trust on the death, in 1850, of Allan Glen, a successful Glasgow tradesman and businessman, 'to give a good practical education and preparation for trades or businesses, to between forty to fifty boys, the sons of tradesmen or persons in the industrial classes of society'. The school's emphasis on science and engineering led to it becoming, in effect, Glasgow's High School of Science. As such, in 1887 its management merged with the nearby Anderson's College to form the Glasgow and West of Scotland Technical College which later became the Royal Technical College in 1912, the Royal College of Science and Technology in 1956 and ultimately the **University of Strathclyde** in 1964.

Hutchesons' Grammar School was a charitable foundation dating back to 1643 and was situated on Crown Street in Gorbals for much of its history. Boys coming into the school in the nineteenth century, usually at the age of 8, received four years' elementary schooling before being apprenticed to a trade. This changed in 1872

Education

Pupil from Wilson's School, Glasgow. (Glasgow University Archives, MS Murray 593)

when moderate fees were charged and schooling provided up to university entrance standard. In 1876 a girls' school was opened in the former Gorbals Youth School in Elgin Street, moving to Kingarth Street in Pollokshields in 1912.

The **Glasgow High School for Girls** was founded in 1894 and housed variously in Garnethill and Kelvindale to serve the area north of Sauchiehall Street which had developed into a lower middle-class residential area. It was probably the largest girls' school in Scotland originally aimed at 'the children of less wealthy parents'. **Park School** started in 1870 as a boys' school in Lyndoch Place, Park Circus, and becoming a girl's school ten years later and joining with two other Glasgow girls' schools in 1976 to form the West of Scotland School Company. One of the other two was the **Laurel Bank School,** founded in 1903 and by 1919 established in a group of converted terraced houses in Lilybank Terrace. The second was **Westbourne School,** begun in 1877 to 'educate young ladies' and based in a terraced house in Westbourne Gardens.

UNIVERSITIES

The **University of Glasgow**, founded in 1451, is the fourth-oldest university in the English-speaking world and one of Scotland's four ancient universities. By the eighteenth century a student had a father in trade, commerce or the professions rather than a working or labouring class background; but even this contrasted with the socially top-heavy landed gentry and aristocratic student bodies in the English universities. More than half of the students at the University of Glasgow between 1740 and 1830 came from middle-class backgrounds. Most of the students lived in bare and comfortless college chambers, though a few wealthier boys boarded with the regents or in private houses with 'masters', who might give them extra-mural tuition. Gowns were worn not only in college but also on the public streets. Speech, even informal conversation, was allowed only in Latin.

Glasgow Caledonian University (informally GCU or Caledonian or Caley) was formed in 1993 by the merger of the Queen's College, Glasgow (founded in 1875) and Glasgow Polytechnic (founded in 1971). The **University of Strathclyde** is Glasgow's second university by age, being founded in 1796 as the Anderson's Institute, and receiving its Royal Charter in 1964 as the United Kingdom's first technological university. The university was founded in 1796 through the will of John Anderson, Professor of

Education

Natural Philosophy at the University of Glasgow, who left instructions and the majority of his estate to create a second university in Glasgow which would focus on 'Useful Learning' – specialising in practical subjects – 'for the good of mankind and the improvement of science, a place of useful learning'.

KEY SOURCES
Glasgow City Archives hold records of schools under the jurisdiction of local authorities, including non-denominational and Roman Catholic schools. It also has a limited number of records for fee-paying schools. It has records for schools, pupils and teachers from more than 300 school board or local authority schools, mainly in Glasgow, but also some for the county areas.

School records mainly consist of admission registers and log books:

- Admission registers: these are the main source of pupil information and can contain the following information about each pupil: name, date of birth, address, date of admission and date of leaving. Some registers contain sensitive information about pupils, for example, the results of IQ tests. These registers are closed for seventy-five years.
- Log books: these are journals kept by the headteacher and include information such as staff and pupil absence figures, fire drills and visitors to the school. Some log books include comments about teachers and pupil teachers (trainee teachers). However you very rarely find information about individual pupils within these records. As log books may contain sensitive information, these are closed for fifty years.

Teachers
Glasgow City Archives also hold records relating to teachers and pupil teachers employed by the local school boards (later the

Glasgow Education Authority and then the Glasgow Corporation Education Department). The records include:

- List of masters and mistresses at day schools, Glasgow School Board, 1874–1918.
- Register of pupil teachers, Glasgow School Board, 1878–98.
- Teachers appointment book, Glasgow School Board, 1878.
- Ex-pupil teachers' appointment and particulars as to changes in staff, 1880–1904.
- List of ex-pupil teachers, Glasgow School Board, 1898–1902.
- List of teachers on military service, Glasgow School Board, 1917–18.
- Register of teachers, Cathcart School Board, 1905–17.
- Register of teachers, Govan School Board, 1873–88.
- Teacher record cards, Glasgow Corporation Education Department, arranged by year of leaving, 1913–85.

These records are closed for seventy-five years under the Data Protection Act (1998).

There are no admission registers or log books online, but some photographs of school buildings and classrooms are available on the Virtual Mitchell website at http://www.mitchelllibrary.org/virtualmitchell/.

The **St Mungo's College of Medicine** roll book, 1891–1917 (DC 246/3/1) is on the Glasgow University website at http://www.gla.ac.uk/media/media_410387_en.pdf.

The records of the **Glasgow School of Art**, fifteenth century–2014, include student records, 1881–1997 and are held in its Archives and Collections Centre.

University of Glasgow
The names of graduates of the university up to 1912 can be found on the University of Glasgow Story at http://www.universitystory.gla.ac.uk/alumni/.

Lord Rector of Glasgow University. (Glasgow University Archives, MS Murray 593)

The following printed books containing the names of graduates and matriculated students up to 1897 are available in many major libraries:

- W. Innes Addison, *A Roll of the Graduates of the University of Glasgow from 31 December 1727 to 31 December 1897* (Glasgow, 1898). (Available online).

- W. Innes Addison, *The Matriculation Albums of the University of Glasgow from 1728 to 1858* (Glasgow, 1913).
- *Munimenta Alme Universitatis Glasguensis. Records of the University of Glasgow: from its foundation till 1727*, 4 vols (Glasgow: [Maitland Club], 1854). Index in Vol. 4. Students are listed in Vols 2 and 3 (available online). The index of names (and a list of the regents – the early teaching staff) (available online).
- W. Innes Addison, *Prize Lists of the University of Glasgow from Session 1777–78 to Session 1832–33* (Glasgow, 1902).

University of Strathclyde

The University Archives are the official records of the University of Strathclyde, documenting its history from its foundation in 1796 as Anderson's Institute. The types of records in the University Archives include student reports, staff records and examination papers. For more details see http://www.strath.ac.uk/archives/universityarchives/.

Glasgow Caledonian University Archive

The university archives' collections contain material on a wide range of subjects including Scottish left-wing politics, trades unions, campaign and pressure groups; Scottish social work, social policy and child welfare; Scottish public health; Scottish social enterprise; and the university's contribution to the development of Scottish higher education from the late nineteenth century onwards. It also houses the records of the university and its parent bodies (dating back to 1875 and the formation of the Glasgow School of Cookery). See http://archives.gcu.ac.uk/.

Newspapers are an invaluable source for those wishing to study the numerous educational establishments that sprang up in Glasgow during the eighteenth and nineteenth centuries. They include advertisements from schools seeking staff or pupils, as well as accounts of prize days and sports day. According to the *Scottish Guardian*, 26 July 1853, a teacher from Glasgow Academy

Education

supplemented his modest income by taking in boarders: 'MR BELL, ENGLISH MASTER of the Glasgow Academy, respectfully intimates that he has accommodation for a few Young Gentlemen as BOARDERS, at his resident, 4, Kew Terrace, opposite the Botanic Garden.' Advertisements can provide an interesting insight into the nature of the city at the time. On 19 August 1891 Langanside Academy and Boarding Establishment, 'A High-class School for Young Ladies and Gentlemen' near Queen's Park, declared that 'it is a very healthy district for delicate children or those suffering from asthma'.

Chapter 10

HEALTH AND WELFARE

The local authorities in Glasgow were faced with enormous social problems as the rapidly growing city suffered from appalling social poverty, crime and disease. The massively unequal distribution of wealth meant that the splendid mansions in the West End were a marked contrast to the wynds and closes of the High Street, Saltmarket and Gallowgate areas in the East End. Here an estimated 20,000 people were crammed into dilapidated housing and sanitation was virtually non-existent. William Mitchell, in his *Rescue the Children* (1886), stated that a third of families lived in one room:

> In some rooms may be found a superfluity of articles – old beds, tables, chairs, boxes, pots, and dishes, with little regard to order or cleanliness. In others, a shakedown in the corner, a box or barrel for a table, a broken stool, an old pot or pan, with a few dishes. In many rooms, no furniture at all; and the whole family, including men, women and children, huddled together at night on such straw or rags as they can gather.

The reality of the slum was brought home to the public in 1842 by the *Reports on the Sanitary Condition of the Labouring Population of Scotland*, produced under the direction of Edwin Chadwick. In the wynds of Glasgow Chadwick found the inhabitants 'worse off than wild animals which withdraw to a distance and conceal their ordure', and that they actually hoarded their own dung to help pay the rent:

Health and Welfare

The interiors of these houses and their inmates corresponded with the exteriors. We saw half-dressed wretches crowding together to be warm; and in one bed, although the middle of the day, several women were imprisoned under a blanket, because as many others had on their backs all the articles of dress that belonged to the party were then out of doors in the streets.

Overcrowding was only part of the problem, and disease was rampant. Tuberculosis, typhus, scarletina, whooping cough, smallpox and measles left a trail of death and misery. In the 1860s two-fifths of all deaths in Glasgow were due to respiratory diseases and tuberculosis. The age group most vulnerable to death by illness was the very young. Deaths of children under 10 accounted for more than half the deaths in Glasgow in the early nineteenth century, and even as late as 1861, 42 per cent of all deaths in the city were in this age group. Most vulnerable were children born in one-room homes ('single ends'). Of all the children who died before this age in Glasgow 32 per cent were born or living in single ends, while only 2 per cent were in five-roomed homes.

The city's trade connections with the Empire soon brought a new plague – cholera. The first epidemic occurred in 1832, killing 3,000 in Glasgow. The appearance of cholera brought a greater degree of urgency for those in authority to tackle disease and it causes. What made cholera so influential was its deadliness; 50 per cent of those who contracted the disease in 1832 died. Another reason was the fact that it struck at all social classes. A further cholera epidemic in Glasgow in 1847–8 saw the first steps taken to improve public health standards.

Dr James Burn Russell, one of Glasgow's pioneering medical health officers, realised that the filthy environment was promoting the spread of disease and he used the new registration information to help persuade Glasgow's City Fathers and rate-payers to fund an ambitious scheme to bring a clean water supply into the city from Loch Katrine. This scheme combined with Glasgow's new sewage system, of which 50 miles was laid between 1850 and 1875, began to ease the health and sanitation problem in the city. By the 1890s Glasgow had more municipal services than any other city of its size. Beside these improvements, the fall in the price of basic foods in the 1870s and 1890s, the improvement of milk supplies, free school meals and the widening influences of nurses, midwives and health visitors were just as important in cutting back death rates among the poor as cleaner water and more efficient sewerage systems.

From the 1840s the Police Acts allowed the municipal authority some power to intervene to improve sanitation, control overcrowding and to demolish decayed buildings. However, it was not until 1866 that the City Improvement Trust was set up to clear away and improve a number of narrow and dirty courts, lanes and streets in the crowded residential areas of the old city centre, mainly around the Gallowgate, Saltmarket, Trongate and the High Street for development by private builders. In the 1870s, the trust also cleared away the old Gorbals village and redeveloped the area to form the new Gorbals Cross, at the same time developing new workers' tenements around the former Oatlands Square.

The first half of the twentieth century witnessed major improvements in access to public health provision. Just prior to the First World War important legislation was passed in the form of the Education Act of 1908 which included compulsory medical inspections of schoolchildren. Local authorities were empowered to provide food and even clothes for those children who were classed as either poor or needy. The success of the authorities in improving health provision is seen by the fact that although tuberculosis still remained one of the most important causes of death, infectious disease such as typhus, scarlet fever and smallpox had all but been nearly eradicated by the early twentieth century.

POOR LAW

After the Reformation in 1560 until 1845, the responsibility for the poor fell on the parish, jointly through the heritors (local landowners) and the Kirk sessions. Each parish was responsible for

Health and Welfare

An inmate of Glasgow City Poorhouse. (Glasgow University Archives, MS Murray 591)

their own poor, i.e. those who had settlement there, either through birth, marriage or length of residence. The type of assistance given was generally outdoor relief, providing clothing, food, goods or money, and poorhouses or their equivalent were often funded by local Scottish merchants.

A Commission of Inquiry was set up in 1843 to decide how to reform the Poor Law system. This resulted in the 1845 Scottish Poor Law Act being passed which established parochial boards in parishes and towns and a central Board of Supervision in Edinburgh. Provision of poor relief in Glasgow was divided into four parishes: City, Barony, Govan and Gorbals, with each to have its own workhouse. In fact, Gorbals never set up a workhouse and was absorbed into Govan in 1873.

While the guardians were legally responsible for the management of the workhouse and the collection and expenditure of money, the day-to-day running of the workhouse was carried out by a number of salaried officials. The staff consisted of a master, matron, clerk, chaplain, schoolmaster, medical officer, porter and additional assistants and servants that the guardians deemed necessary. The Scottish Poor Law aimed to enforce discipline. The rules of the Glasgow poorhouse laid down that, 'All the inmates . . . shall rise, be set to work, leave off work, and go to bed at such times, and shall be allowed such intervals for their meals as the House-Committee shall direct – and these several times shall be notified by the ringing of a bell'. The instructions issued to all workhouses by the Board of Supervision in Edinburgh in 1850 stated that:

> Before being permitted to communicate with the other inmates, the poor person shall be thoroughly cleansed, and shall he clothed in a Poorhouse dress, and the clothes which such poor person wore at the time of admission shall be purified, and deposited in a place appropriated for that purpose, with the owner's name and a list of the articles affixed thereto, and such clothes shall be returned when the poor person leaves the Poorhouse.

Records

Each district kept detailed registers of the poor receiving relief while the board also kept minutes of meetings and accounts of assessments and expenditures. Not all records survive equally well,

but those that do are very helpful to family history research.
Glasgow City Archives hold registers for the following areas:

- Glasgow, 1851–1948.
- Barony, 1861–98 (part of Glasgow from 1899).
- Govan, 1876–1930 (part of Glasgow from 1930).
- Bute, West Dunbartonshire, South Lanarkshire, Renfrewshire (not Paisley), often dating from 1845.

A return of the most destitute families and individuals within the police jurisdiction of Glasgow was prepared by the Police Superintendent, 1841, and can be viewed online at the City Archives website. The NHS Greater Glasgow and Clyde Archives holds records of Govan Poor House Hospital Infirmary.

HOSPITALS

Although great progress was made in improving the environment and the water and sanitation systems, provision also had to be made for those who succumbed to disease and ill-health. Unless one was a pauper, all health care at this time had to be paid for privately. In 1733 the town council built the Town's Hospital, which was partly a workhouse, partly a hospital, partly a place of refuge for the elderly and partly an orphanage. A small number of minutes of the Town's Hospital, of which the volume for 1741–3 lists applicants for poor relief, are held by the Glasgow City Archives.

By the nineteenth century if a person was ill there were three types of care available: treatment at a voluntary hospital; treatment in a Poor Law hospital; and treatment at home by a doctor. The voluntary or teaching hospitals were supported by private donations, endowments and subscriptions. To receive treatment a patient had to be provided with a 'line' signed by a subscriber. All patients had to leave the hospital within forty days, and funeral expenses were to be guaranteed by the subscriber. Certain categories of patient were not admitted – the poor, as poorhouses dealt with them, apprentices and servants, who were to be looked after in their masters' houses.

This Valentine & Sons postcard dating from 1932 shows the Royal Infirmary main building with the cathedral to the right.

There were also some illnesses considered unsuitable for entry, including those associated with pregnant women and incurable diseases such as smallpox.

From 1845 the very poor and those suffering from incurable diseases were treated by the Poor Law hospitals. As treatment was financed out of the rates the managers of the hospitals were under pressure to keep expenditure down. From the 1850s to 1870s operations for the removal of tumours were performed in the patient's own bed or on a table in the ward as there were no funds for separate operating rooms. Those on poor relief could also receive visits from the parish doctor and call at his surgery free of charge. This outdoor medical service was, however, stretched to the limit. In the city parish of Glasgow in 1875 one doctor was employed for every 20,000 of the population.

It was not until the nineteenth century that the problems in Poor Law hospitals were addressed. In Glasgow there was a hospital

Health and Welfare

building programme initiated which did much to relieve the pressure of overcrowding. The programme allowed for the separation of the hospitals from the poorhouses, and those with minor illnesses from those with chronic ones.

Hospital Records

Hospital records are mainly held in the NHS Greater Glasgow and Clyde Archives. The records consist primarily of the records of hospitals, clinics and asylums in Glasgow, Dunbartonshire, Greenock and Paisley. These include the records of **Glasgow Royal Maternity Hospital**, registers, 1834–1981 and case notes, 1866–1921; records of **Royal Beatson Memorial Hospital**, registers of admissions and discharges, 1894–1988; Records of **Belvidere Hospital**, admission registers, 1865–1965; staff registers, 1878–1950; and records for the **Glasgow College of Nursing and Midwifery**, register of nurses and female servants, 1877–1902; **Glasgow Royal Infirmary**, attendance registers, 1893–1918.

Asylums

The Glasgow City Archives holds a number of records relating to lunacy including:

- Records of Glasgow District Lunacy Board, 1888–1944 (Ref. D-HEW7) which include registers of boarded-out mental patients, records of petitions for certification and registers of notified cases.
- Lunatic asylum record books, 1943–62 (Ref. D-HEW35).
- Particulars of cases visited in regard to lunacy certificates, 1949–62 (Ref. D-HEW36).
- Records of Renfrew District Lunacy Board, 1858–1948 (Ref. CO2/8/1) including minute books and a register of pauper patients in Dykebar Asylum.
- Registers of lunatics in Govan Combination Parish, 1877–1930 (Ref. D-HEW5/2).

Woodilee Hospital was the largest parochial asylum in Scotland with 400 inmates. The **NHS Greater Glasgow and Clyde Archives** holds correspondence regarding patients, 1919–56; post-mortem reports, 1881–1956; records of official inspections, 1877–1955; admission warrants, arranged by date of death or discharge, 1924–61; annual reports, 1883–1919; case notes, 1875–1956; registers of admissions, discharges and deaths, 1875–1992; registers of accidents, 1879–1956; registers of escapes, 1879–1962; and registers of staff, 1874–1978. There is a 75-year closure on records of adults and a 100-year closure period on records of minors.

You can access a list of the NHS Greater Glasgow and Clyde Archives holdings online at http://www.archives.gla.ac.uk/gghb/collects/hospital.html.

Chapter 11

MIGRATION

Between 1750 and 1821 Glasgow's population exploded from just under 32,000 to over 147,000 people. Unlike other cities whose populations grew consistently and stably over time, Glasgow's growth was so rapid that from 1800–30, it was a city largely composed of newcomers. As John Tait, editor of the *Liberator Newspaper*, noted in his evidence to the select committee which examined the state of the Irish poor in Great Britain in 1836, 'There are few persons you meet in Glasgow who can say that their fathers were born in the town'.

By the second half of the nineteenth century the population of the Scottish Highlands was declining rapidly. Like their counterparts in the Lowlands, they left their native parishes as agricultural changes forced them off the land towards the opportunities and uncertainties of city life. Highland migrants often followed other locals or fellow parishioners to cities such as Glasgow where they settled in the same areas. The proportion of Argyll-born Highlanders in Shettleston and Maryhill, for example, was higher than for the city as a whole and large numbers of migrants from Bute settled in St John's parish. The Revd Dr Norman Macleod confirmed this to the Poor Law commissioners:

> I think the Highlanders find it more easy to get respectable employment than the Irish; the Highlanders have many friends in Glasgow to whom they can apply. They come with letters of recommendation to countrymen and clansmen who are in comfortable circumstances; we are very clannish; and

Workers with their shuttles at Marquis Street Weaving Factory, c. 1890. (Glasgow City Council, Glasgow Museums)

those who come from one Island do it for the men from that Island who have to get employment – the Macdonalds for the Macdonalds and the Macleods for the Macleods and so on, so that they find very little difficulty in getting work.

Highlanders were employed in mills and as manual labourers but also in skilled occupations such as printing, coopering, inn-keeping and in textiles. In Glasgow several Highlanders became prominent industrialists, including Robert Macfie, Greenock's sugar refinery, Archibald Campbell, in the glassworks there in 1793, and probably the most notable, George Macintosh, who, by 1777, had established the Dunchatten dye works at Dennistoun, on the north-east outskirts of Glasgow. All the employees were Highlanders and a role call was taken in Gaelic every morning.

From the late eighteenth century, Glasgow was a natural place of settlement for Irish Protestants, particularly Presbyterians, who shared a common ancestry and cultural heritage with Lowland Scots. Unfortunately, census records do not distinguish Irish immigrants by religion and Protestant numbers can only be calculated by subtracting where they can be identified from the number of Catholics from figures for the Irish as a whole. The census of Glasgow in 1831 made by James Cleland, for example, revealed 35,554 Irish out of a total population of 202,426, but only 19,333 were listed as Catholics. It has, nevertheless, been estimated that a quarter of Irish immigrants to Scotland during the nineteenth century were Protestant.

There were also significant links between the textile and shipbuilding industries in Belfast and Glasgow. Skilled in linen handloom weaving, many came to work in the cotton weaving communities in the villages round Glasgow, such as Calton and Bridgeton. In 1834, Bishop Scott of Glasgow remarked that 'almost all the Irish in this city and neighbourhood come here from the northern counties of Ireland'. Irish Protestants also brought with them a commitment to the Orange Order and by 1835 there were twelve lodges in Glasgow. The Orange Order often gave support to the newly arrived immigrants with groups such as the Glasgow Orange Union Funeral Society and the Glasgow Ulster Society. By the 1850s Ulster Protestants established specifically Protestant areas such as Govan where they would later become closely identified with Rangers Football Club.

Unskilled Irish Catholics came to the west of Scotland from the 1750s in large numbers to undertake the heavy physical work involved in improving farm land. A quickly expanding industrial city needed such labourers in large numbers and they began to settle in the less favoured parts of Glasgow. Unlike cities such as Manchester and Liverpool, the Irish did not stick to their own quarter in Glasgow. Moses Steven Buchanan, senior surgeon at Glasgow Royal Infirmary, observed in 1836, 'There are no streets in Glasgow exclusively inhabited by Irish – there is no street where you would not probably find more than an equal population of Scotch along

Workmen leaving by the main gate of the Fairfield Shipbuilding and Engineering Co. works.

with them – they appear to be quite amalgamated and mixed up with the poor population of the town'.

During the late 1840s the potato crop failed across the whole of Ireland, and that failure was repeated in successive years. Many starving and destitute people fled to the industrial towns on the British mainland. The *Glasgow Herald* described it in June 1847 as 'The Irish Invasion' and complained that:

> The streets of Glasgow are at present literally swarming with vagrants from the sister kingdom, and the misery which many of these poor creatures endure can scarcely be less than what they have fled or been driven from at home. Many of them are absolutely without procuring lodging of even the meanest description, and are obliged consequently to make their bed frequently with a stone for a pillow.

It has been estimated that as many as 8,000 per week arrived in Glasgow at the height of the famine. By 1851 over 30 per cent of the

'Irish-born' in Scotland were based in Glasgow, and they constituted 18 per cent of the city's total population.

Irish Men, women and children provided cheap labour in the textile industry, chemical works, potteries and tobacco factories. Many men were employed as unskilled labourers in mines, iron and steel works, docks, locomotive works and the construction industry, so that the terms 'navvy' and 'Paddy' became synonymous in the public mind despite one estimate that only 10 per cent of 'navvies' were actually Irish by birth.

The Catholic Irish were often depicted by newspapers, politicians and Poor Law commissioners as drunken, idle and lazy. Robert Gillespie, in *Glasgow and the Clyde* (1876), painted a fairer picture when he noted:

> The population [of Glasgow], as is the case in Liverpool, contains a large Irish element. This is estimated at from a fifth to a fourth of the entire community. But the Irish abroad seem to differ materially from the Irish at home. In Glasgow, they are remarkable chiefly for their steady industry, and they are just as peaceably disposed as the Scots among whom they live. It is quite astonishing to find how many succeed in establishing themselves in business as small dealers, and how often they thrive in pursuing avocations in following which a Scot or an Englishman would never be able to keep his head above water. Numbers find Glasgow a sort of El Dorado, in which they acquire a sum of money equal to a fortune in their estimation, and return to the Green Isle to settle down in comfort with the battle of life more than half won.

The Irish in Glasgow were faced with a lack of priests in the city during the first half of the nineteenth century and adapted to their new surroundings by marrying with the local population and dropping the Irish forms of their surnames. As numbers grew, and more priests were available to minister to them, neighbourhoods became organised around the parish with its church, school and branch of the Society of St Vincent de Paul offering assistance to the needy. On a wider scale the sense of a Catholic community was promoted by newspapers such as the *Glasgow Observer*, which provided religious, political, sporting and cultural news for the Irish Catholic population. An important development was the foundation of Celtic Football Club in 1888 by a Marist brother, Brother Walfrid, as a focus for the recreational energies of Catholic young men. Four years later the Gaelic Football Association imposed a ban on soccer and other 'foreign sports' being played by its Irish membership, but the expatriate Irish Catholics in Glasgow had built up such enthusiasm for the game that they refused to comply with the ruling and Celtic Football Club became a powerful symbol of Irish Catholic sporting success in Scotland.

One major group of migrants that is often neglected is the Lowland Scots, who came from the surrounding countryside. Life in the countryside, even in the better years, was hard and stern and the scarcity of money was everywhere apparent to travellers as they journeyed north of the border. Only a minority of the rural population held a lease, with many of these holding only a few acres of land. By the middle of the eighteenth century more enterprising landlords began to combine small tenancies into one farm and let to more substantial tenants who came under agreement, with a lease of nineteen years. Although there was often violent opposition, most of those evicted from their holdings accepted their position stoically, taking work on the labour-intensive farms or fleeing to growing industrial towns like Glasgow. John Tait told the select committee in 1836:

> A large part of the population of Glasgow consists of Scotch from the Lowlands. Taking Glasgow as a centre, there are persons who have come to it from all sides, with a circuit of sixty miles; my father originally came from the Lothians, and had been a country farmer; he was driven out by the improvements in farming, became a mechanic, and settled in Glasgow; most of my acquancies either were born in the country, or their parents came directly from the country . . .

Migration

John Tait was probably not far off the mark when he assessed the make-up of Glasgow a decade before the Great Irish Famine as 'divided into five parts, of which the native inhabitants would be one fifth, the lowlanders two fifths, the Highlanders one fifth and the Irish one fifth'.

The rise of Glasgow's permanent Jewish community, mainly merchants and traders, took place during the nineteenth century. The first recorded reference is to an Isaac Cohen, hatter, who was admitted burgess and guild brother in September 1812. By 1823 there were sufficient Jews in the city to set up a small community which met for worship in a little synagogue in the High Street.

For much of the nineteenth century Jews settling in Glasgow had been largely shopkeepers and businessmen, many of them from Holland or Germany, but in the 1870s and 1880s large numbers of Jews from Russia and Poland fled persecution in their homeland. Another reason was that one of the biggest warehouse concerns in Glasgow, Arthur & Co., introduced new methods of bulk tailoring, and recruited largely among the London Jewish tailors. Jewish hawkers and peddlers were also highly visible on Glasgow's streets.

Between the 1890s and the outbreak of the First World War the Jewish population of Glasgow swelled from about 2,000 to nearer 6,000, most of the increase coming from Eastern Europe. The main area of settlement was Gorbals in Glasgow, where an estimated 6,500 had settled by 1901. Gorbals was attractive because of its cheap accommodation, but once roots had been established and individuals began to prosper there was a movement towards Pollokshields.

For much of the eighteenth and nineteenth centuries Italians came to Glasgow, and these were largely educated skilled and artistic people. The skilled craftsmen who set up their businesses included Antoini and Gallati, the carvers and gilders who established their firm in Glasgow in 1805, and Gerletti, who manufactured looking glasses, barometers and thermometers in Glasgow during the 1820s. It was not until the second half of the

Members of the Crolla family collecting blocks of ice from the factory of ice merchants R. White in Laird Place in Bridgeton during the 1930s. (Glasgow City Archives)

nineteenth century that Italian immigrants arrived in large numbers and these were largely unskilled peasants such as the Barghigiani, who settled in Glasgow and the south-west of Scotland. During the mid-nineteenth century the population of Barga experienced increasing poverty due to the fact that their small farms were no longer viable. They arrived in Glasgow where they found Italians from the Ciociari district who were already laying the foundations of a successful ice-cream industry. The Barghigiani followed their example and established fish and chip shops. By the turn of the century families from Barga were running some of the most prestigious restaurants in Glasgow and a pattern of chain migration was established. In addition to catering, Italians found themselves involved in hairdressing. Through their role as barbers and

Migration

hairdressers they established the College of Italian Hairdressers in Glasgow in 1928.

Italians initially established themselves in areas like Partick and Garnethill in the West End of Glasgow. It is estimated that by 1905 there were 5,000 Italian immigrants in Glasgow. Italian migration declined during the 1920s and 1930s because of the Aliens Order in 1920 which required immigrants to have a work permit and the rise of Fascism in Italy which brought to power a government that resisted the large-scale emigration of its people. The outbreak of war resulted in the targeting of Italian shops in Glasgow, which was compounded by the arrest of all Italians males between the ages of 17 and 60 as potential enemy agents.

Although Glasgow had strong links with Asia from the eighteenth century, there is no direct evidence of an Asian community in the city. There is little doubt that sailors and traders would have had a conspicuous presence in the dockland area during the height of the Empire but by 1919 white seamen objected so strongly to their employment that rioting broke out in the Broomielaw, and 130 black seamen were forced to leave the city. According to the *Dundee Courier*, 25 January 1919:

> The affray began in the yard of the Merchant marine Offices, where a heated dispute developed into furious fighting between white and coloured sailors and firemen. Revolver shots were fired, and knives and sticks freely used . . . A large and hostile crowd of British seamen and white sailors of other nationalities followed the coloured men to their lodging-house in the neighbourhood, to which they ran for refuge . . . Great excitement prevailed among the beleaguered men, who, it is stated, fired from the lodging-house windows several shots at their opponents gathered outside on the Broomielaw.

By the 1920s Indian immigrants were visible on the roads as hawkers, mainly of clothes, and few areas of the city were without its own 'Indian Johnny'. Others followed and in 1937 the Indian

Association was set up in Glasgow. Many found work in wartime factories during the Second World War and, such were their numbers that they established the Muslim Mission in a temporary mosque in Gorbals in 1940. They lived in the streets just south of the Clyde which had been vacated by the city's Jewish community.

After the war numbers continued to grow and by 1960 about 3,000 were living in Glasgow. Many found employment as drivers and conductors in Glasgow Corporation tramcars and buses – at one time they formed more than half the workforce. In 1984 the Muslim community opened the first custom-built mosque in Scotland on the south bank of the Clyde with accommodation for some 2,000 worshippers. Today over 50,000 Asian migrants call Glasgow home and are grandparents to second-, third- and fourth-generation Asian Scots. The Pakistani Muslim community is now the biggest ethnic group in Glasgow with approximately 30,000 people.

The Chinese community in Glasgow dates from the 1950s and are mainly Cantonese from Hong Kong New Territories and their descendants. They came at the direct invitation of the corporation, and many originally found employment in the city's hospitals. The first Chinese restaurant in Glasgow was the Wah Yen in Govan Road, opened by Jimmy Yih in the late 1940s. Now almost all work in the catering trade.

RECORDS
Glasgow City Archives holds the historical records of Strathclyde Police and its predecessor forces. Statistics were published in the City of Glasgow Police Chief Constable's annual reports from 1938 onwards and early immigrants from Russia, mainland Europe, America, Scandinavia and Egypt are recorded as having registered with the Aliens Registration Department. Later statistics demonstrate the growth in immigrants from further afield travelling to Strathclyde from Africa, Asia and South America. Few alien registration records survive but the following are available:

Migration

- Argyll County Constabulary alien registration and transfer cards, 1917–75 (Ref. SR22/91/73).
- City of Glasgow Police Nationality Branch, register of aliens, 1962–75 (Ref. SR22/63/25).

Before the First World War there was no requirement for a person travelling abroad to apply for a passport. The vast majority of those travelling overseas had no formal documentation and passports were mainly held by people with certain occupations, such as merchants. During this time Glasgow had the power to issue its own passports. Glasgow City Archives holds registers of passports issued by the city between 1857 and 1914 (Ref. B8/23/1). A database of people who applied for passports is available in the archives' searchroom. In many cases this includes occupations, other members of the family travelling, home address and destination.

Glasgow City Archives holds the records of Glasgow Corporation's Office for Belgian Refugees, 1914–19. The Glasgow Corporation was appointed as the distributing centre for Scotland for Belgians escaping the German invasion of their country. The records include several lists relating to 8,000 Belgian refugees to Scotland, 1914–15 (Ref. D-CA12/2-4) as well as a record of the burial place of Belgian refugees who died in Scotland, 1914–19 (Ref. D-CA12/1). Indexes to the lists of Belgian refugees sent to Scotland are also available online at www.glasgowfamilyhistory.org.uk/. School admission registers are also a useful source of information as local authorities were responsible for educating the children of Belgian refugees.

During the First World War aliens resident in Britain and belonging to Allied nations had either to return to their own country to undertake military service or become liable to serve in the British forces, unless they were granted a certificate of exemption by their home country ambassador or a tribunal. The City of Glasgow Town Clerk's Department was granted authority from the War Office to hear tribunals of those who applied for exemption from military service. Only one list of around 130

Russian tribunal applicants survives, dating from 1917 (Ref. D-TC19/box3).

The Scottish Jewish Archives Centre

Founded in 1987 and based in Garnethill Synagogue, it preserves catalogues and displays the records of the Jewish community of Scotland from the eighteenth century. The centre houses a museum display on the history of Jews in Scotland.

Chapter 12

GLASGOW AT WAR

Because of its geographical location, Glasgow did not enjoy the same sort of prominence in Scotland's early military history as Edinburgh or the major strongholds at Stirling and Dumbarton. Although there was a castle, the Bishop's Palace, there was never any proper city walls or other fortifications. Glasgow sent a contingent of its citizens to fight at the Battle of Flodden (1513) under the command of Matthew, Earl of Lennox, the city's Provost. Like most of Scotland's aristocracy, he was killed at the battle which ended in catastrophic defeat. Just over 50 years later the city sent a contingent of 600 men to join with the 4,000-strong army of the Regent, the Earl of Moras, to defeat the forces of Queen Mary at Langside on 13 May 1568. It was said that the Regent was so pleased with the support he received from Glasgow that he granted its baxters (or bakers) the Partick Mills which from then on were known as the Regent Mills.

Glasgow was spared any direct involvement in the Civil War, although it became a military centre for the royal forces against the Covenanters after the Restoration of Charles II. After the removal of the Catholic King James II and his replacement by the Protestant William of Orange and Mary, Glasgow supported the new regime and as the seventeenth century progressed it became strongly Hanoverian. During the Rising of 1745, the Whig, anti-Jacobite burgesses of Glasgow supplied only £5,000 in cash and £500 in kind in response to the Jacobite demand for £15,000 cess or land tax (about £2 million at today's prices). Meanwhile, the professors at the University of Glasgow combined to pay the wages of a pro-Hanoverian company of fifty soldiers.

From 26 December to 3 January 1746, the army of Prince Charles Edward Stuart spent a week in Glasgow after his retreat from England, but gathered little or no support. He was unenthusiastically received by the Whig citizens, as Provost Cochrane reported: 'Our people of fashion kept out of his way; few or none at the windows; no ringing of bells, and no acclamation of any kind . . . Our ladies had not the curiosity to go near him, and declined going to a ball held by his chiefs'. On 17 January Glasgow Militia fought alongside government forces at the Battle of Falkirk where they suffered heavy casualties in a Jacobite victory.

Glasgow also demonstrated its loyalty during the American War of Independence. Private and public subscriptions raised within the city enabled a full regiment to be established in 1777 for service abroad. This was the 83rd Regiment of Foot or the Royal Glasgow Volunteers. The attraction of the regiment was no doubt helped by the £30 bounty offered to recruits – the equivalent of about two-and-a-half year's pay for a private. Later that year the 83rd was transferred to New York, where it remained as part of the garrison of the city until the end of the Revolutionary War in 1783. It then returned to Glasgow, where it was disbanded.

To the citizens of Glasgow, the army was a constant presence in the city. Before the establishment of an efficient police force, urban unrest until the first half of the nineteenth century was maintained by the use of military force, both infantry and cavalry. More than half of the forty or so units stationed in the city during the nineteenth century were English and half a dozen were Irish – the Iniskilling Dragoons visited the city eight times between 1824 and 1880 and the Irish Regiment of Foot four times between 1786 and 1850. The remainder were Scottish and almost every Scottish infantry or cavalry unit was stationed in the city at one time or another. The coming and going of these regiments was reported in detail in the local newspapers: According to the *Greenock Advertiser*, 16 January 1855: 'On Thursday forenoon the first division of the 2nd (Royal Lancashire) Regiment of Militia arrived in Glasgow by Railway, and marched to the barracks in the Gallogate, preceded by the band, which played some lively airs. It is now half a century since Glasgow was garrisoned by an English militia regiment.' These regiments were based at **Maryhill Barracks** from 1872. The barracks replaced the previous infantry barracks at Duke Street in the East End of the city, which dated from 1795.

Newspapers provide an invaluable source for those interested in Glasgow and its regimental history. They offer an interesting insight into military life in the eighteenth and nineteenth centuries and can reveal some interesting genealogical information. The *Glasgow Herald* of Friday, 7 February 1866 includes a detailed description of a deserter from the Glasgow Highland Volunteers:

> DESERTED
> From the GLASGOW HIGHLAND VOLUNTEERS, without delivering up their clothing, etc.
> KENNETH STEWART, Drummer, and
> DANIEL McLEAN, Private
> Kenneth Stewart is by trade a weaver, aged 27 years, five feet six inches high, brown hair, and round visage; talks the Gaelic language; and commonly wore a short brown coat and corduroy breeches.
> Any person who will give information where the Deserters can be found, will receive, on their being seized, a suitable reward from the Commanding Officer of the Regiment.

THE HIGHLAND LIGHT INFANTRY

The Regiment most associated with Glasgow is the Highland Light Infantry. It was formed in 1881 with the amalgamation of the 71st (Highland) Light Infantry (as the 1st Battalion) and the 74th (Highland) Regiment of Foot (as the 2nd Battalion) as the city regiment of Glasgow. Both these regiments were Highland units, but the new unit was made the county regiment of Lanarkshire, primarily recruiting in Glasgow. Seperately and together, the regiment's predecessors and the new regimement took part in all the major and minor outbreaks of hostility from the eighteenth to

Maryhill Barracks c. 1908.

the twentieth centuries, including the American Revolutionary War, the Crimean War, the Indian Mutiny and the two world wars. On the outbreak of the First World War the regiment rapidly expanded until in reached almost thirty battalions. The Glasgow Corporation raised two battalions. The first of these, 1st Glasgow (15th Battalion) was made up almost entirely of recruits who worked for the city's tram service. The 2nd Glasgow (16th Battalion) was formed from former members of the Boys' Brigade. In similar fashion the members of the 3rd Glasgow (17th Battalion) were drawn from the Glasgow Chamber of Commerce. Most of the original recruits for the 17th were students of the Royal Glasgow Technical College, former pupils of local schools (including the High School and Glasgow Academy) and white-collar workers from the business houses and different trades of Glasgow and the surrounding area. There were also a number of battalions made up from Milita and Volunteer forces, most of which were disbanded at the end of the war. The Terriotial Army furnished two battalions which existed until after the Second World War.

The Highland Light Infantry saw action on the Western Front and in Mesopotamia and Gallipoli. 2nd Battalion deployed straight to the Western Front on the outbreak of the First World War, remaining there throughout the conflict. In contrast, 1st Battalion only arrived on the Western Front in December 1914, moving to Mesopotamia (modern Iraq) in January 1916 and remaining there for the rest of the conflict. The regiment also raised fourteen Territorial battalions and eleven Reserve and Service battalions between 1914 and 1918. Three of the Territorial battalions were sent to Gallipoli in 1915. A total of about 80,000 Glasgow men served in the Highland Light Infantry during the First World War, and of these, more than 10,000 were killed.

In 1923 the regiment's title was expanded to the **Highland Light Infantry (City of Glasgow Regiment)**. During the Second World War the regiment saw action in many different engagements. The 2nd Battalion had been in Egypt on the outbreak of the Second World War before fighting in North Africa, Sicily, Italy, Syria and the Balkans and serving as peacekeepers in Greece for the last four months of 1944. In 1945 the Battalion joined the occupation force in Austria, moving back to Greece later that year.

The Highland Light Infantry continued in service until it was amalgamated with the Royal Scots Fusiliers in 1959 to form the **Royal Highland Fusiliers (Princess Margaret's Own Glasgow and Ayrshire Regiment)**.

For more information on the regiment and its predecessors, it is worth visiting the website of the **Highland Light Infantry Association City of Glasgow Regiment** at http://www.highland lightinfantry.org.uk/.

EARLY MILITARY RECORDS

Before the Union troops were raised as and when needed. The threat of a French military invasion and the lead up to the Napoleonic Wars led to the re-establishment of the Scottish Militia by the Militia Act (Scotland) of 1797. Under the Act, Lord Lieutenants raised Militia forces within each county for national defence. A survey or ballot of all men between the ages of 18 and 45 (between 18 and 30 before 1802) was carried out and from these ballots those who actually served were selected. It was possible for a balloted man to nominate a substitute to serve in his place. Some groups were exempted such as apprentices, schoolmasters, ministers and some paupers.

Officers were usually members of the local gentry or pensioned officers who had served in the regular army. Members worked in their normal occupations until called out, and unlike the Volunteers they did not drill regularly. In the 1850s, almost every Militia regiment was mobilised for home defence in order to release regular army regiments to fight in the Crimean War (1853–6) and to suppress the Indian Mutiny (1857).

The records of Glasgow Corporation include:

- Reports on the City Guard containing lists of guards, 1790–1 (D-TC12/2).
- Register of Glasgow Militia certificates and orders of aliment for wives, 1810, 1813–16 (D-TC12/1).

Muster rolls of Militia and Yeomanry (volunteer forces) are often found among the family papers of the leaders of these troops. The City Archives holds many collections of these family and estate papers, which include a small number of these records. You should check with the archives to see whether there are any of interest to you.

The records of the Glasgow Militia, 1810–31 are available online, http://www.glasgowlife.org.uk/libraries/the-mitchell-library/archives/collections/online-resources-for-archives/.

The NRS holds muster rolls of troops stationed in Scotland, 1667–1732.

SERVICE RETURNS

The returns of Scots who died in military stations abroad have been digitally imaged as part of the Statutory Records of Scotland. Copies of these images, together with a full index, are one of the many

Churchill Tanks of the 6th Guards Tank Brigade and Highland Light Infantry.

resources available as part of the **ScotlandsPeople** network which you access in the Registrars within the Mitchell on payment of a daily fee. The service returns include records of deaths of:

- Army returns of deaths of Scottish persons at military stations abroad (1881–1959).
- Service departments registers of deaths outside the United Kingdom of persons ordinarily resident in

Scotland who are serving in or employed by HM Forces, including families of members of the forces (1959–present).

FIRST WORLD WAR RECORDS
Evening Times Roll of Honour
During the First World War, the *Evening Times* newspaper printed short biographies of service personnel from Glasgow and the surrounding areas who were reported missing, wounded or killed, often as an appeal from their families for further information. Entries usually include regiment, address, family names, occupation and often a photograph. This photograph may be the only one that exists of the person at that time. The rolls of honour are available online at the City Archives website at http://www.glasgowfamilyhistory.org.uk/ExploreRecords/Pages/Evening-Times-Roll-of-Honour.aspx.

Glasgow Corporation Rolls of Honour
Glasgow Corporation produced rolls of honour to commemorate those who died in the First and Second World Wars. These contain the name, rank, regiment and address of thousands of people who died during the conflicts, although they are not completely comprehensive.

The City Archives holds copies of the following rolls:

- First World War (Ref. C5/9/1).
- Second World War (Ref. C5/9/2).
- Second World War, civilian dead (Ref. C5/9/3).

In addition to these the City Archives holds rolls for some other areas, including:

- Rutherglen, First and Second World Wars (Ref. RU4/6/126).
- Cambuslang, First World War (Ref. CO1/63/6/4).

Rolls of honour were also created by other types of organisations, such as businesses, trade incorporations and schools. The Archives hold a number of these rolls. Occasionally schools produced rolls. If your ancestor was employed by a particular company or was a member of an incorporation, it is always worth checking whether the Archives hold any such rolls of honour. Examples of these include:

- David Black & Co., wholesale merchants and clothing manufacturers, First World War (Ref. TD1422/20/9).
- Incorporation of Bonnetmakers and Dyers, First World War (Ref. T-TH15/13).
- Albert Road Academy, First World War (Ref. TD398/1).
- Camlachie Public School, First World War (Ref. D-ED7/35/14).
- Glasgow University, Second World War (Ref. T-TH1/101/4).

The **Registrars at Glasgow City Archives** hold war returns of deaths of Scots for various conflicts, including those for the First World War. The war returns have been digitally imaged and indexed. Copies of the digital images and indexes can be accessed as part of the ScotlandsPeople network at the Registrars in the Mitchell on payment of a daily fee. Also available here are soldiers' wills and the records of Military Service Appeal Tribunals.

An absent voters' roll for Glasgow dated 1920, but which includes men who had fought in the First World War, is available at the City Archives. Standard electoral rolls for other areas in Strathclyde may also refer to men absent due to them serving in the war.

The war returns, soldiers' wills and Military Service Appeal Tribunal records can be accessed online at the ScotlandsPeople website on payment of a fee. The original First World War service records are held at The National Archives (but can be accessed online via Ancestry).

SECOND WORLD WAR RECORDS

The Registrars hold war returns of deaths of Scots for various conflicts, including those for the Second World War. The war returns have been digitally imaged and indexed. Copies of the digital images and indexes can be accessed as part of the ScotlandsPeople network during a visit to the Registrars at the Mitchell.

Glasgow Corporation and other organisations produced rolls of honour to mark the contribution of those who died in the war. The City Archives hold those rolls published by the council:

- Second World War (Ref. C5/9/2).
- Second World War, civilian dead (Ref. C5/9/3).

The Clydeside Blitz

On the nights of 13 and 14 March 1941, more than 250 German bombers attacked factories and shipyards on Clydeside. High-explosive and incendiary bombs rained down, devastating buildings and resulting in large numbers of fatalities, especially in the town of Clydebank. For more information visit https://www.blitzonclydeside.co.uk/index.aspx?articleid=2263.

The Glasgow City Archives hold the records of the Civil Defence Department of Glasgow Corporation, which includes:

- Registers and other records of persons killed or injured in air raids, 1940–1.
- Messages and reports, including air-raid incidents and situation reports, 1939–44.
- Map showing areas of bomb damage to the city in 1941 (Ref. D-AP8/14). If your ancestor's property was affected by bombing during the SecondWorld War, it may be shown on the map.

Evacuees

The Department of Health in Scotland spent the early months of 1939 preparing details for the evacuation of unaccompanied children, mothers with children under school age, blind people and invalids from vulnerable areas. Areas affected were Edinburgh, Rosyth, Glasgow, Clydebank, Dundee, Inverkeithing and Queensferry – and from May 1941, after the Clydeside air raids, Greenock, Port Glasgow and Dumbarton were added.

Evacuation was voluntary. Some had made private arrangements but when the order came at 11.07 on 31 August 1939 to 'Evacuate Forthwith' nearly 120,000 left Glasgow within 3 days for Perthshire, Kintyre and Rothesay. Stirling was one of the first areas to receive evacuees. The state of the Glasgow children who were evacuated to Stirling led to a government inquiry. Councillor Hay told Stirling Town Council's monthly meeting that 'on the night after the evacuees arrived those dealing with them would willingly have become evacuees themselves to escape from the hundreds of frantic householders asking what they were going to do about ridding them of the lice and filth which had invaded their homes'. He went on to claim:

> The evacuation scheme might be termed the greatest social experiment of our generation. At any rate it had been the biggest shock the public has received since the early industrial revolution. It has lifted the veil on the lives of thousands of the populace, disclosing squalor, disease, dirt and ignorance of the elementary laws of health and decent living that had appalled those of us who have had to cope with it.

The expected Nazi blitzkrieg, however, did not materialise, and by January 1940 around three-quarters of the evacuees had drifted back to Glasgow. After Clydeside was heavily bombed for the first time in 1941, some 58,000 schoolchildren were evacuated again, joining the 20,000 who had stayed in the country.

The Glasgow City Archives hold a file from the Glasgow Corporation's Civil Defence Department about its general arrangements for the evacuation of Glasgow schoolchildren. This includes a list of Glasgow schools where children might be

Evacuees, Glasgow Herald, *24 February 1941.*

evacuated from, as well as guidance notes for parents about evacuation. However, individual children or families that were evacuated are not named.

The City Archives also holds log books and admission registers for many Glasgow schools and a large number for schools in the west of Scotland. Information about evacuees is most likely to be found within school log books (journals kept by the headteacher). Entries in the log books usually state where and when children were evacuated, and how many were evacuated. However, in most instances the names of the children evacuated are not given. Sometimes teachers who accompanied children are named. Very rarely a school admission register will include a note that a pupil was evacuated, as well as when and where they were evacuated. Additionally, the City Archives hold registers of persons evacuated to the Burgh of Oban, which includes many Glasgow children.

Chapter 13

SPORT AND ENTERTAINMENT

For much of the city's history Glasgow's working class took its entertainment on the street where entertainers, most often ballad singers or fiddlers, collected coppers, and street characters such as Hawkie (a wit) and Malabar (a juggler) were popular. The public house was also popular, ranging from grand saloons to illegal shebeens. Alexander Brown left an account of Sunday night in Glasgow after the Forbes-Mackenzie Act of 1853 had closed licensed premises on the Sabbath. Bridgegate was filled with crowds of men, women and children: 'Rows of women, with folded arms – scarcely a broken link in the chain for long distances together – line the inner side of the pavement'. The only drink available was at an illegal shebeen where 'the landlord of the private drunkery' gave 'a glass of very good ale' for 'a very good price, too'. Monday night was worse with 'the idiotical jeer and senseless laugh of drunkards, the horrid oaths and imprecations of low prostitutes . . . nearly every shop on both sides of the street is a public house . . . Rags, povery, disease and death are the appropriate emblems of the district'.

On the other hand, not all leisure activities in Glasgow were drink-related. Some institutions, such as the Tontine Coffee House and Hotel, prohibited alcohol and tobacco. The large number of city bookshops and subscription libraries indicated more contemplative habits. A visitor to Glasgow in July 1794 was impressed by the Tontine Coffee House and Hotel: 'A grand bow, lighted by five lofty sashes' projected into the court of the hotel.

Houdini, Pavilion Theatre, Thursday, 3 June 1920. ((c) Herald & Times *Group)*

Sport and Entertainment

On entering, we found a room of seventy or eighty feet in length with corresponding dimensions of height and breadth, having another small window on one of its sides mingling its auxiliary light with those of the bow. This was no other than the great subscription coffee-room, supported by certain annual conscriptions of more than six hundred of principal citizens of Glasgow, and members of the university. Half the newspapers of London, and Gazetteers from Ireland, Holland and France, and a number of provincial journals, and chronicles of Scotland and England, beside reviews, magazines, and other periodical publications, are objects of the subscription. At the daily arrival of the post, a more stirring, lively, and anxious scene could hardly be imagined. But no part of the day passes without some concourse of subscribers, or of strangers at the hotels whom their liberality permits freely to partake the benefit of the rooms.

The early nineteenth century saw greater restriction on casual games on Glasgow Green and in the streets, accompanied by a reaction against activities such as cock-fighting and dog-baiting. Nonetheless, Glasgow got a new cockpit in 1835 with accommodation for 280 people. Swimming in the river seems to have been the most popular sport in the 1830s, but as the Clyde became more polluted enthusiasm dwindled. With the opening of a pool in **Alexandra Park** in 1877 and the opening of both private and public baths over the next two decades interest revived, notably with women bathers increasing in the early years of the twentieth century.

As the population density of Glasgow grew the authorities took the provision of open spaces extremely seriously, with the result that the town council purchased land in the 1850s for parks such as **Queen's Park** and **Kelvingrove Park**. **Glasgow Green**, situated in the East End of Glasgow on the north bank of the River Clyde, is the oldest park in the city, having been established in the fifteenth century. The park served a number of purposes in its first few centuries; as a grazing area, an area to wash and bleach linen, an area to dry fishing nets and for activities like swimming. The city's first 'steamie', called The Washhouse, opened on the banks of the Camlachie Burn in 1732. An area of land, known as Fleshers' Haugh was purchased in 1792 by the city, extending the park to the east. In 1817 and 1826, efforts were made to improve the layout of the park. Culverts were built over the Calmachie and Molendinar burns and the park was levelled out and drained. In 1855 the St Andrew's Suspension Bridge was opened, connecting Glasgow Green to the north and Hutchesontown to the south. The bridge was constructed to replace an existing ferry crossing and allow workers from Bridgeton and Calton to reach factories in Hutchesontown.

The **People's Palace and Winter Gardens**, situated in Glasgow Green, was opened on 22 January 1898 by the Earl of Rosebery. At the time, the East End of Glasgow was one of the most unhealthy and overcrowded parts of the city, and the People's Palace was intended to provide a cultural centre for its citizens. At the opening ceremony Lord Rosebery called it: 'A palace of pleasure and imagination around which the people may place their affections and which may give them a home on which their memory may rest'. He declared the building 'Open to the people for ever and ever'.

Two of Scotland's oldest sporting clubs, Clydesdale Amateur Rowing Club (est. 1857) and Glasgow University Rowing Club (est. 1867, now known as Glasgow University Boat Club), are situated on the banks of the River Clyde at Glasgow Green. Clydesdale ARC moved from the south side of the river to Glasgow Green in 1901.

Although there were festivities at New Year, Glasgow Fair, which was held at the Green at the foot of the Saltmarket before it moved to Camlachie in 1871, was the main holiday of the year. Until the 1960s most local businesses and factories closed on 'Fair Friday' to allow workers and their families to attend, typically spending their time in the Firth of Clyde or on the Ayrshire coast. This practice was known as going 'doon the watter'. This became popular after the 1840s when steamers were sufficiently large and numerous to make it possible for significant numbers of people to travel to the coast. In

This scene, photographed by Thomas Annan in 1895, features the steamers Daniel Adamson *and* Benmore *moored in the foreground and the* Iona *canting in midstream. Postcard published by the Reliable Series.*

1840 the Glasgow & Greenock Railway opened, enabling Glasgow people to join boats at Greenock. From this date sailing to Dunoon and Rothesay became central to the experience of the fair. The Victorian villas at Dunoon and the ones that stretch around Rothesay Bay were built for business and professional families to spend a few weeks by the sea.

As the nineteenth century progressed and industry in Glasgow grew, there was a notable improvement in conditions for the skilled and semi-skilled worker. For these workers Glasgow offered a variety of options, as Robert Gillespie, author of *Glasgow and the Clyde* (1876), commented:

> if rents and provisions are now considerably higher, present wages ... allow the... the artisan's household to live in a style

to which they were formerly strangers. They have comforts and even luxuries at their disposal. They are better clad and better housed than they were formerly, and wife and bairns as well as father can afford to spend a week or two at the 'saut water' during the season. In town, they have a Free Library for purposes of either amusement or instruction. There is a Mechanics Institute, and lectures are frequent during the winter in various institutions. Concerts at a cheap rate are given in the City Hall every Saturday evening, and entertainments of the same class are repeatedly produced in other districts. Then, of course, there are the theatres and music halls which are freely patronised, though it is a singular fact that it is impossible to fill the boxes of the former unless during the brief season of Italian Opera.

The first theatre in Glasgow was built in 1764 on the present-day site of Central station. But like many theatres it was burnt down by religious mobs. Acting, especially for women, was considered scandalous and thespians often had to be escorted to and from the venues. The **Theatre Royal** is the oldest surviving theatre in Glasgow, located at 282 Hope Street in Cowcaddens. The theatre originally opened in 1867, the name changing to the Theatre Royal in 1869.

In 1845, despite public protest, Britain's largest theatre, the **City Theatre**, seating 5,000, was built on Glasgow Green, but its over-ambitious size led to its closure a few months later.

The **Metropole Theatre** opened in Stockwell Street in 1897, taking over the Scotia Music Hall which had been established in 1862. Sir Harry Lauder, who had made early amateur appearances at the Scotia, became a regular patron of the Metropole in recognition of the opportunities it had given him. But the most famous international star to learn his trade on the Metropole stage was Arthur Stanley Jefferson, whose first stage appearance was at the Panoprican in 1906. His father, Arthur, manager of the Metropole, then let him appear on his stage using the stage name Stan Laurel for the first time.

Sport and Entertainment

Glasgow Empire Theatre, known as the Glasgow Palace Empire until the early 1900s, opened in 1897 on the site of the Gaiety Theatre at 31–5 Sauchiehall Street. The Empire presented variety, revues, musicals and dance, winter circus, pantomimes and ice spectaculars, and especially shows produced by Tom Arnold. Over the years many stars appeared including Lillie Langtry, Laurel and Hardy and Sir Harry Lauder. The Empire was notorious within showbiz circles as 'The English comic's grave', if their act was slow or thin. Comedian Ken Dodd famously disparaged attempts to psychoanalyse humour with the rebuttal, 'The trouble with Sigmund Freud is that he never played second house at the Glasgow Empire after both halves of the Old Firm had just lost!'

Glaswegians have always been keen on the cinema, so much so that in 1939 the city boasted the highest number of seats per capita anywhere in the world. Glasgow's moving picture fascination started in 1896 at the Ice Skating Palace on Sauchiehall Street. Within a year music halls like the Coliseum, the Alhambra and Pickard's Panopticon were incorporating 'films' into their weekly entertainment. Glasgow's first purpose-built cinema was Sauchiehall Street's Electric Theatre, which opened its doors in 1910.

The public house was still the main form of entertainment for working-class men. It was partly in order to draw men out of the pubs that a football association was formed in Glasgow in March 1873. The previous year 154,446 persons had been apprehended in Glasgow for being drunk, incapable and disorderly. On 13 March of the following year, in Dewar's Temperance Hotel in Bridge Street, a group of men met, representing seven football clubs, and decided 'that the clubs here represented form themselves into an association for the promoting of football according to the rules of the Football Association'.

The game quickly flourished and the world's first international football match was held in Glasgow in 1872 at the West of Scotland Cricket Club's Hamilton Crescent ground in the Partick area. The match was between Scotland and England and resulted in a 0–0 draw. Football was a particular passion for the Glasgow working

SEASON 1917-18.

Back Row—J. Nelson, J. Ward, J. Strang (*Secretary*).
Middle Row—J. Nutt (*Trainer*), W. Aitken, D. M. Inglis, F. Wilson (*Assistant Trainer*), H. Duncan, A. Ford, H. Hillhouse, R. Young.
Front Row—K. Mackenzie, R. M. Morton, A. Cowan, P. White (*President*), A. L. Morton, H. Paton, A. Stevenson.

From Richard Robinson, History of the Queen's Park Football Club, 1867–1917 *(1920).*

man, as James Hamilton Muir noted in his book *Glasgow in 1901*:

> His time for enjoyment is short, for his Saturday has only twelve hours, and on the morrow descends the pall of the 'Sabbath' to smother pleasure. His work, too, is hard, and now that he works not with his hands, but in controlling a machine, the demands on his attention have made his work all the more exhausting. As his nights will not serve for recreation, he must crowd into his Saturday afternoon and evening the excitement which shall compensate for a week of labour. So football is his game, for no other can give the same thrill, the same fierce exhilaration, the same outlet for the animal spirits which machinery has suppressed. It is intoxication by the eye, and to

Sport and Entertainment

serve its purpose the game has become the British bull-fight, and has made those who look on at it as brutal and callous as any Spaniards. Sportsmanship vanished alike from players and spectators when the game became a trade, and behind the referee's back everything is permitted. If the offence is committed by his own side the working man will not protest; for it has given him a new thrill. The players are his gods until their powers decline,

Glasgow has three professional football clubs: **Celtic, Rangers** and **Partick Thistle.** A fourth club, **Queen's Park**, is an amateur club that plays in the Scottish professional league system. Celtic and Rangers, popularly known as 'The Old Firm', are the most successful clubs in Scotland, between them having won 101 Scottish League championships (Rangers with 54 and Celtic with 47), 69 Scottish Cups and 42 Scottish League Cups. Queen's Park is the oldest football club in Scotland, having been founded in 1867. It took part in the first ever English FA Cup, entering at the semi-final stage against the famous public-school side Wanderers. The game ended goalless. Unable to remain for the replay due to financial constraints, Queen's were compelled to scratch. They finished runners-up in the FA Cup on two subsequent occasions, in 1884 and 1885, both times to Blackburn Rovers.

Glasgow had six other professional clubs during the late nineteenth and early twentieth centuries: Clyde, which moved to Cumbernauld, Third Lanark, Cambuslang FC, Port Glasgow Athletic FC, Cowlairs FC and Clydesdale FC, which all went bankrupt. Senior teams such as St Mirren, Hamilton Academicals, Clyde, Albion Rovers, Airdrie United and Motherwell play in Greater Glasgow, as well as the long-defunct Abercorn FC.

Bowling was another popular activity with 200 clubs meeting in Glasgow in 1848 and agreeing rules drawn up by the solicitor William Mitchell. Cricket in Scotland is over 200 years old, largely introduced by English soldiers garrisoned in the town. It became popular from the 1830s with the first Scottish championship involving the Glasgow Cricket Club in 1834. The **West of Scotland Cricket Club** was founded in 1862 and the **Clydesdale Cricket Club** in 1848, making it Glasgow's oldest surviving team sports organisation. In its early days Clydesdale also played football and were losing finalists to Queen's Park in the first ever Scottish Cup Final, and in 1870 its members helped to set up the Scottish Football Association. The Club moved from their first ground in Kinning Park to the present ground, Titwood, in 1873. The old ground was sold to a fledgling football club, Rangers FC, with whom the club have maintained strong links to the present day.

Glasgow Golf Club, founded in May 1787, is the ninth oldest golf club in the world. The town council had started to issue permits for playing golf on Glasgow Green some years before and the records of the Kirk session show that golf was being played in Glasgow almost 200 years before. The club has changed location several times during its history, but at the beginning of the twentieth century took out a twenty-year lease on the 100-acre parkland estate and mansion house of Killermont, just 5 miles from the city centre, on the north bank of the River Kelvin (a permanent tenture was secured in 1922). The club is unusual in also having a links course, at Gailes, near Irvine, on the Ayrshire coast, some 35 miles away.

RECORDS
The Scottish Theatre Archive
The Scottish Theatre Archive forms part of the Special Collections Department of the **University of Glasgow Library**. It can be searched online at http://special.lib.gla.ac.uk/sta/search/. Among the largest collections are the archives of the Citizens Theatre, Scottish Ballet, including material from its beginnings as the Western Theatre Ballet, the BBC Radio Scotland script collection and the Jimmy Logan collection of music-hall material. Other collections include items relating to many Scottish theatres and companies, such as the Scottish National Players, Wilson Barrett Company and the Edinburgh Festival Fringe.

Sport and Entertainment

Royal Conservatoire of Scotland Archives & Collections
The Royal Conservatoire is Scotland's national centre of professional vocational training in performance arts. The RCS was originally founded as the Glasgow Athenaeum in 1847, teaching a variety of subjects, including art classes, to students in Glasgow. Their holdings include minute books, prospectuses, student records and photographs which reveal the organisation's history. Visit its website at https://www.rcs.ac.uk/.

Football Archives
The **Scottish Football Museum** is the Scottish Football League's National Museum of Football, located in Hampden Park, Glasgow. The museum houses over 2,000 objects of football memorabilia, including the world's oldest cap and match ticket, from the first official international match of 1872, as well as the world's oldest national trophy, the Scottish Cup, which was made in 1873. For details of its holdings see http://www.scottishfootballmuseum.org.uk/.

If your ancestor played for a particular club it is best to approach the club historian via the team's website. In the case of Partick Thistle, contact Club Historian and Honorary Vice-President Robert Reid, author of the definitive book about the Jags, *Red and Yellow Forever*, who is happy to search through club records to see if your ancestor played for the club; robert.reid@ptfc.co.uk.

Further Reading
Bone, D.D., *Fifty Years Reminiscences of Scottish Cricket* (1898)
Conville, J., *The Glasgow Golf Club, 1787–1907* (1907)
Ferrier, Bob, *McElroy, Robert* (2005)
Ferrier, Bob, *Rangers: The Complete Record* (2005)
Findlay, Bill (ed.), *A History of Scottish Theatre* (1998)
Greig, T., *'The Bully Wee' – being an appreciation of the first hundred years in the history of Clyde, F.C.* (1978)
Hutchison, David, *Glasgow and its Citizens, Scottish Theatre since the Seventies* (1996)
Litster, John, *Third Lanark: Life and Death of the Hi Hi* (2010)

Macaulay, James, *The Glasgow School of Art: Charles Rennie Mackintosh (Architecture in Detail)* (2002)
McNee, G., *The Story of Celtic – An official History 1888–1978* (1978)
O'Brien, Ged, *Played in Glasgow* (2010)
Potter, David and Phil Jones, *The Encyclopedia of Scottish Football* (2011)
Queen's Park FC Souvenir Pictorial 1867–1849 (1949)
Robinson, R., *History of the Queen's Park Football Club 1867–1917* (1920)
Thorburn, S., *The History of Scottish Rugby* (1980)
Whitton, J., *The Public Parks of Glasgow* (1919)
Wilson, Brian, *Celtic – A Century With Honour* (1988)

Chapter 14

LAW AND ORDER

As Glasgow became more industrialised so the centre of the population shifted as those who could afford it moved to spacious suburbs such as the fine terraces in Kelvinside and the villas south of the Clyde. The poor remained in the older parts or were confined in hastily constructed areas often surrounding the mills or factories where they worked. The rapid growth of the city brought with it many social problems which manifested itself in an increase in crime. For much of the nineteenth and twentieth centuries policing and punishment became major concerns for the city authorities.

As people crammed into the city, certain areas became notorious for congestion, disease and pestilence: the area south of the Trongate, Calton, the area west of the Saltmarket and the region near the old High Street contained housing that was among the worst in Europe. The Laigh Kirk Close at 59 Trongate alone housed twenty brothels and three shebeens in 1871. Observers castigated the poor for its criminal habits. Assistant Handloom Weaving Commissioner J.C. Symonds wrote of Glasgow: 'I did not believe, until I visited the wynds of Glasgow, that so large amount of filth, crime, misery, and disease existed on one spot in any civilised country'.

Victorian writers frequently linked crime to immorality and drink. Temperance tracts such as *Moral Statistics of Glasgow* (1849) and *Facts and Observations of the Sanitary State of Glasgow* (1844) set out to prove the link between vice, drink and morality. James Dawson Burns, in his *Commercial Enterprise and Social Progress, or, Gleanings in London, Sheffield, Glasgow and Dublin* [1858], commented:

The duties of the police in Glasgow, are, perhaps, more onerous than in any other town in the United Kingdom. The numerous low dens in the purlieus of the city and suburbs are continually infested with a savage and brutal horde of burglars, who carry on their operations in the most daring manner. There are also a numerous, brood of young thieves, many of whom prowl about the town both day and night with the stealth of cats, in consequence of their enjoying the luxury of bare feet.

The *Scottish Topographical Dictionary*, published in 1845, agreed:

Crime and juvenile delinquency was often linked to drink. The existence of crime in Glasgow may be traced in a great measure to intemperance, and the encouragement to it presented by no fewer than 2,300 licensed public-houses, or other places for the sale of excisable liquors, which exist in the city and suburbs. A vast number of these are tippling-dens of the lowest description; and it is presumed that they might be greatly thinned with infinite advantage to the community.

Juvenile crime also caused panics from time to time and, by the 1860s, Glasgow had four reformatories and four industrial schools for the delinquent young. The first probation officers, including one woman, were introduced in 1905. The House of Refuge opened in 1838, for boys charged with or convicted of crimes. Its objectives were to provide the boys with 'a good plain education, industrious habits and the knowledge of a trade', and thus discourage juvenile delinquency. A Girls' House of Refuge and Reformatory was opened soon afterwards in Parliamentary Road. The Juvenile Delinquency Board also managed an industrial school for boys, an industrial school for girls and a day industrial school, all of which provided food, education, religious instruction and industrial training for destitute children, whether admitted on private application or under a magistrate's warrant.

A Glasgow policeman. (Glasgow University Archives, MS Murray 594)

According to the detailed accounts provided in local newspapers the most common felonies dealt with were burglary, highway robbery and theft of clothes or other personal possessions. The following is a typical entry from the *Glasgow Herald*, 5 February 1806:

GOODS STOLEN

WHEREAS, yesterday forenoon, during Divine Worship, MARY FORD, servant of Lachian McIntosh, Vintner in the Post-Office Court, absconded from his house, carrying with her a large quantity of valuable Wearing Apparel, and, among other articles, a Black Velvet Bonnet. Any person giving such information at the Herald Office, as may lead to her apprehension, will be handsomely rewarded; and any person harbouring her after this published notice, will be prosecuted according to law. Mary Ford is 16 years of age, tall, fair complexioned, and came lately from Dumfries.

Towards the end of the nineteenth century gang violence became more common. In the overcrowded slums violence was part of day-to-day existence. Seeing safety in numbers, those youngsters who survived childhood sought comradeship, protection and excitement through violence. The **Penny Mobs** was the name used by the press to describe the street gangs active in Glasgow during the early 1870s. As the court system offered heavy fines as an alternative to imprisonment, gang members were often freed after a collection from the gang at a 'penny a head', which is where the name came from.

Although the gangs declined after courts no longer offered fines for offenders, the smaller gangs eventually banded together for mutual protection which gave rise to the prominent gangs of the early twentieth century such as the Tongs, the Billy Boys and the Norman Conks. In Glasgow these gangs were strongly sectarian in outlook. The Brigton Boys, also called the Billy Boys of Brigton Cross, were a Protestant street gang led by Billy Fullerton. The gang often clashed with Catholic gangs such as the Norman Conks (or Norman Conquerors), which was a large Catholic street gang active from the 1880s to the 1960s, with its headquarters and most of their members based around the Catholic area of Norman Street in Bridgeton.

POLICING

Before the formalisation of the police force in Glasgow, law was

Law and Order

upheld by the Kirk sessions, which took action against those deemed guilty of breaking the Sabbath or taking the Lord's name in vain. In 1779 the Burgh of Glasgow met to 'consider the expediency of appointing a fit person to be inspector of the Police of the City of Glasgow'. This predated Robert Peel's London Metropolitan Police by twenty-nine years but the force failed through lack of finance in 1781.

During the following eleven years, Glasgow city fathers tried to get their Police Bill before Parliament, but without success. In the meantime, the local authorities had again to rely on a city guard of citizens.

The Glasgow Police Bill finally received Royal Assent on 30 June 1800. This enabled the town council to set up the **Municipal Police Board**, which was responsible for fire fighting, lighting, cleansing, controlling taverns and dram shops, and paving. Police powers in Glasgow were extensive: the system of ticketed houses allowed the police to search working-class homes without a warrant. In a single year in Glasgow, 55,000 'night inspections' revealed only 7,000 houses breaking the overcrowding law, about 13 per cent of these investigated.

The activities of the Police Board were reported extensively in the local newspapers. At the weekly meeting held in the Police Buildings, the *Glasgow Herald* of 10 September 1847 reported that:

> The Clerk read a petition from the proper tiers and tenants in North Frederick Street, representing the annoyance which they suffered from large numbers of boys and girls being allowed to assemble in that street, especially on Sunday evenings, when they were accustomed to make much noise, ring house-bells, and otherwise contact themselves in a manner subversive of order and of the respect due to the Lord's-day.

The local inhabitants were highly critical of the lack of action taken by the police, as were members of the board. Mr McClean, a member of the board, claimed:

there was a class of vagrants at present going about to whom the attention of the police ought to be particularly directed, These were the bone-gatherers, persons who came about closes, stairs, and entries, upon frivolous errants, and who were believed to be in communication with blackguards who had other objects in view. He would recommend to the inhabitants that all persons found prowling about lanes for the purposes of picking up bones and rubbish, should be handed over to the police.

Also under the 1800 Glasgow Police Act, John Stenhouse, a city merchant, was appointed Master of Police and he set about organising and recruiting the force. He appointed three sergeants and six police constables, dividing them into sections of one sergeant and two police constables to each section. On 15 November, the Glasgow Police mustered in the Session House of the Laigh Kirk, Trongate, for the first time. There were three reliefs. One sergeant and two police officers were on duty in the police office for 24 hours, the other section on patrol duty and the third entitled to rest for 24 hours. The sixty-eight watchmen were also there in their long brown coats with their personal numbers painted on their backs. Each carried a lantern and long stave. They would man fixed points within the city while the police officers patrolled to prevent crime. According to the *Scots Magazine*, 1 January 1807:

> In Glasgow, all the watchmen have fixed stations, at a small distance from each other, to which they remain invariably attached. By this means the whole city is kept constantly under their eye; no part of it is ever destitute of an officer of police. On the least tumult arising in any quarter, the nearest watchman instantly rings his bell; the same thing is done by the two next to him, by whom it is repeated; thus every man successfully gives the alarm to his neighbours, and presently police officers pour in from all quarters, in sufficient numbers to overwhelm any band of rioters who are likely to be collected in one place.

Law and Order

Superintendent of the Gorbals Police, George Jeffrey, told a select committee that the normal procedure was all persons apprehended 'are taken to the police office, and brought before the magistrate; and as I attend as procurator fiscal, crimes of a serious nature are remitted to the sheriff'. He had no doubt who the main perpetrators or the cause of the crime were likely to be:

> Of the persons brought before our Court, I should suppose that about two-thirds are Irish, principally for assaults, for being drunk and disorderly, and, in general, for breaches of the peace. The great proportion of these takes place on the Saturday night or Sunday morning. The Irish fight both in the streets and in the houses, generally with their fists, and only occasionally with weapons; sometimes very serious wounds are inflicted in these encounters. The Scotch mix occasionally in these affrays, but the rows of the Irish are chiefly among themselves, betwixt the Catholics and Protestants.

In 1846 the Glasgow Police merged with the Gorbals, Calton and Anderston Burgh Police. As a result of this, Glasgow Police was divided into 4 divisions and now numbered 360 officers. Following the City of Glasgow Act 1891, the city boundaries were extended to the south, north and west sides of the city. Due to this extension, a system of fourteen cast-iron police signal boxes was installed in the outlying areas. By 1900, the City of Glasgow Police numbered 1,355 officers and men.

On 5 November 1912, by Act of Parliament, the boundaries of the city were again extended and the force merged with the Govan and Partick Burgh Police. In the First World War 300 Glasgow police officers enlisted in the armed forces. As a result, the force employed 400 temporary constables and increased the Special Constabulary to 3,000 to guard strategic buildings and factories within the city. Another innovation was the appointment of Miss Emily Miller as Glasgow's first policewoman in September 1915.

In 1975, the City of Glasgow Police, Lanarkshire Constabulary,

Renfrew and Bute Constabulary, Dunbartonshire Constabulary, Argyll County Police, Ayrshire Constabulary and a small portion of Stirling and Clackmannan Police were amalgamated to create Strathclyde Police. The Glasgow City Archives' holdings include the Strathclyde Police archive and its predecessor forces, including the City of Glasgow Police and the County Constabularies of Ayrshire, Argyllshire, Dunbartonshire, Renfrewshire and Bute, and Lanarkshire.

Police Records
A few criminal registers, photographic criminal registers and photographic convict registers survive within the police records held at Glasgow City Archives. The following are for the City of Glasgow:

- Register of prisoners photographed, liberated between 1919 and 1921 (Ref. SR22/61/25).
- Register of salmon poachers, *c.* 1960 (Ref. SR22/61/27).
- Register of criminals photographed, 1910–33 (Ref. SR22/63/11).
- Photograph album of criminals, 1911–12 (Ref. SR22/63/12).
- Photograph albums of convicts, *c.* 1934 and *c.* 1930 (Ref. SR22/63/19 and 20).

Records are subject to closure periods under the Data Protection Act (1998).

Glasgow City Archives holds record books from the police city mortuary dating from May 1935 to January 2012. The record books do not include post-mortem reports. Due to the sensitive nature of these records, advance permission for access is required.

The **River Clyde Police** was established in 1858 and was responsible for policing the Clyde up to the Tail of the Bank. They were merged into the Marine Police division of the City of Glasgow Police in 1866, and wore a small anchor on their collar. The cost of the division was borne by the Clyde Navigation Trust.

Law and Order

Glasgow City Archives hold the archive of the Clyde Navigation Trust which includes the records of the Clyde Pilotage Authority, 1856–1998; Clyde Lighthouses and Cumbrae Lighthouse Trusts, 1755–1966; Ardrossan Harbour Co., 1886–1968; and Greenock Harbour Trust, 1755–1966.

PRISONS

Before custodial sentences became the general method of punishing criminals, those awaiting trial were housed in the Tolbooth's few apartments. In 1635 the magistrates opened a House of Correction for vagrants and 'dissolute women' in the converted Manse of the Prebend of the Drygate. Inmates were obliged to work at such occupations as spinning, weaving or shoemaking, and the resulting profits went towards the expenses of the institution. A temporary bridewell came into use in 1788 in part of a granary at Shuttle Street and College Street which housed mostly women and boys. A custom-designed Bridewell was erected in about 1798 in the gardens of the old House of Correction which had seventy-four debtors' cells and fifty-eight felons' cells. In 1814 increased jail accommodation was provided in the new Justiciary Court House at the foot of the Saltmarket, facing Glasgow Green.

When the Gaol Act of 1823 assimilated the functions of bridewells and jails, the city, in co-operation with Lanark County, decided to build a new prison, **Duke Street Prison** (again in the grounds of the old House of Correction in Duke Street), which took both the city's convicted criminals and those from the Lower Ward of Lanarkshire. Mrs McMillian, matron of the prison, felt that the neglected childhoods of many of the prison population were to blame for their misdemeanours. According to the *Report on Scottish Prisons* (1846), she was of the opinion that:

> A large number of the female prisoners who have come under my care. I believe that the majority are illegitimate and have been much neglected in their youth; and many of the others have lost one or other of their parents, sometimes both, while

they were very young; and in many cases were exposed to unkind usage by a stepmother or stepfather.

For many orphan children prison offered accommodation and something to eat. A boy 'named P.N.' gave an account of his unhappy childhood which was reported in the *Glasgow Herald* on 18 September 1846:

My father and mother died soon after each other, when I was 12 years old. No one looked after me. At first I went about carrying gentlemen's luggage; but sometimes I could get no job and had nothing to eat. I then began to steal, and ever since have been chiefly living by begging and stealing. I have not been out of prison a fortnight together for three years . . . All the clothes that I have I got from the prison for over-work; but sometimes I am obliged to pawn them.

As Duke Street prison held women prisoners from around Scotland, many Suffragettes and political activists were imprisoned there and their protests over the living conditions would eventually lead to the closure of the esablishment in 1955. Between its first prisoners arriving in 1798 and 1872 various improvements were made to the structure but not to the terrible living conditions, which were mentioned in the Glasgow street song sung to the tune of 'There Is a Happy Land'.

>
> There is a happy land,
> doon Duke Street Jail,
> Where a' the prisoners stand,
> tied tae a nail.
> Ham an' eggs they never see,
> dirty watter fur yer tea;
> there they live in misery
> God Save the Queen!

Law and Order

Executions were carried out at the prison from 1865 until 1928. In 1923 Susan Newell became the first woman to be executed in Scotland for over fifty years. She had strangled a newspaper boy who would not give her an evening paper without payment. She refused the traditional white hood when she climbed on the gallows. She was the last woman to be executed in Scotland. The prison was demolished in 1958 to make way eventually for the Ladywell housing scheme, which was built on the site from 1961–4 and stands to this day. The only remaining structure of Duke Street Prison is some of the boundary wall.

By the 1840s Glasgow had eight prisons including the **Glasgow Green Prison** (known as 'Burgh' or the Southern Prison) which closed in 1863; the Calton Bridwell (used as both a house of correction and lock-up); the prison of Rutherglen (used as a burgh prison, both for criminals and debtors); the prisons of Gorbals and Anderton; and the police prison at Glasgow. **HM Prison Barlinnie** was built in the eastern suburbs of the city in 1882. It consisted of 5 accommodation halls which were built in stages between 1882 and 1897, with each holding approximately 200 inmates. An investigation at Barlinnie Prison found, according to the *Glasgow Herald* of 23 June 1899, 'an examination was made into 245 cases of the prisoners with the longest sentences, and who therefore might fairly be presumed to be the greatest criminals. According to their own statements, 171 of them were more or less affected by liquor at the time when the crime was committed, whilst only 74 were sober.' Inside prisoners were expected to work at tasks such as baking, basket-weaving, blacksmithing, tinsmithing, plumbing, carpentry, shoemaking and mattress-making. Outside, there was labour in the quarry to break up stones for use in extending the prison. Some were not put to work and were destined for the gallows instead. Barlinnie's Hanging Shed only opened in 1946, replacing a gallows at Duke Street Prison, and ten men were executed there before 1960.

Prison Records
The NRS of Scotland holds the prison records from the Scottish

Prison Service and earlier bodies which had responsibility for prisons, including the Prison Commission for Scotland and the Scottish Office Home and Health Department. The main records are the prison registers (HH21), which generally note particulars of the trial and sentence for each inmate as well as personal details such as place of birth, occupation, age, height and religion. The NRS records are for: Barlinnie Prison, Glasgow, 1882–1960 (Ref. HH21/70/1-157) and Glasgow (Duke Street), 1845–1955 (Ref. HH21/32/2-166).

Glasgow City Archives hold the look book for Pollokshaws Industrial School (Ref. D-ED7/281).

THE JUDICIAL SYSTEM

When Scotland was united with England in 1707 it retained its own laws and legal system. Scotland kept its own system of courts, which differed from the English, Welsh and Irish systems, and instead of having barristers and solicitors Scotland retained its advocates and writers. Until modern times Glasgow hosted a wide variety of courts, the oldest of which was the **Burgh Court** which came into being in the Middle Ages when the Bishop of Glasgow was the territorial Lord of Glasgow and its judges were his bailies. Cases were passed from the Kirk sessions to the burgh courts and included adultery, fornication, irregular marriage and witchcraft.

At first the burghs were governed through the burgh courts, originally a gathering of 'all the good men of the community'. Gradually the burgh court meeting in a judicial capacity came to consist of the bailies only, while the town council (Provost, bailies and councillors) attended to the administrative business. They dealt with a wide range of more minor offences. According to the *Glasgow Gazette*, 6 April 1850, Bailie Philips disposed of rather more than the average number of cases for that week including: 'Margaret Thomson, charged with being drunk and disorderly on Sabbath morning, and with abusive and blasphemous language in court. Sentence, 30 days' imprisonment.' On the same day, 'Several persons were fined for wheeling barrows on the foot pathments; several carters for riding on their carts without double reins and bits in their horses' mouths; and

Law and Order

a house-factor was fined 2s.6d. for having the back premises of a property under his charge in a fifthly state'.

The **Sheriff's Court** could adjudicate in all cases of capital crime except the four pleas of the Crown – murder, rape, robbery and fire-raising. The court met from May to June and from November to March in the Old Tolbooth at the Cross until 1814, after which it moved to the new Justiciary Buildings at the foot of the Saltmarket. In about 1844 it moved back to the city centre, to the County Buildings in Wilson Street. According to the *Glasgow Herald* of 18 November 1879, 'Adam McLeish was charged with having, on 17th October, feloniously entered the Inland Revenue Duty Free Warehouse in Warroch Street, by breaking a pane of glass of a window in the office, and stolen a coat and a jacket. There were two previous convictions, and sentence of ten months' imprisonment was imposed.'

Cases requiring judgment by a superior court came before the **High Court of Justiciary on Circuit**. Twice a year itinerant Lords of Justiciary from the central courts in Edinburgh held court in Glasgow and their solemn procession along the Gallowgate from their lodgings in the Saracen's Head Inn to the Tolbooth was a recognised part of the city's ceremonial year. The court dealt with a wide range of cases including theft, housebreaking, serious assault, embezzlement and murder. More unusually, the *Glasgow Herald* reported on 28 December 1888 that John Baird Murdoch, 'a respectable-looking young man' was charged with assault following a football match in Glasgow. Murdoch had come in to Glasgow from Arbroath and after the match had met friends in a restaurant in West Nile Street. The party was turned out at 11, whereupon a quarrel arose on the street and the prisoner 'without any provocations, rushed at a man who was standing looking on, and with a knife stabbed him in the eye, which he gouged out of the socket and irretrievably injured'. In sentencing the young man to twelve months' imprisonment, the Lord Justice Clerk said that 'he could excuse a little violence in moments of excitement, but to use a knife was most un-British indeed'.

Records

The **Glasgow City Archives** hold an incomplete series of burgh court books for Glasgow and Rutherglen. Burgh courts had jurisdiction over various civil and criminal matters. The burgh criminal courts usually dealt with minor matters. Glasgow Burgh Courts records comprise:

- Services of Heirs, 1625–1866.
- Justices of Peace Court, 1663–80.
- Register of Deeds, 1625–1973 (also printed indexes for the rest of Scotland, 1665–83).
- Small Debt Court, 1773–1817.
- Licensing Court, 1779–1977.
- Criminal Court, 1802–1950.
- Police Courts, 1805–75.
- Central Police Court, 1906 (final sitting) (Ref. B3/1/1/1-10).

For the Rutherglen Burgh Courts the records comprise:

- Court, 1619–1975.
- Service of Heirs, 1794–1860.
- Registers of Deeds, 1628–1736.

Glasgow City Archives also holds records of the Justice of the Peace Courts for the nineteenth and twentieth centuries, including minute books, small debt courts and juvenile courts (sometimes incomplete) for the following:

- Dunbartonshire, 1728–1975 (Ref. JP6).
- Glasgow, 1889–1974 (Ref. JP22).
- Lanarkshire (includes Glasgow), 1811–1970 (Refs CO1/10/5/1 and JP16).
- Renfrewshire, 1859–1971 (Ref. JP7).

Among other things, the Justice of the Peace Courts include:

Law and Order

- Licensing courts including applications, appeals, testimonials in favour of applicants and records relating to the type of premise licensed.
- Court books including petty sessions to try small crimes and juvenile courts to deal with young offenders. Such registers usually give the parties' names, the charge, the date of trial and sentence.

A small series of police court records survive and include:

- Glasgow Police Court books, 1813–24 (Ref. B3/1/1/1-10).
- Printed list of cases for trial at Glasgow Autumn Circuit, 1825 (Ref. SR22/53/1).
- Circuit court indictments, 1896–1977 (Ref. SR22/53/2-3).
- Glasgow Sheriff Court book: criminal indictments, 1815–19 (Ref. SR22/53/5).
- Last sitting of the central police court, Glasgow, 1906 (Ref. SR22/63/50).

Further details can be found in contemporary newspaper accounts of the proceedings of the Police Court. The *Glasgow Evening Post* of 30 December 1870 reported:

> Robert Gray, cab driver, pleased guilty of being intoxicated while in charge of a horse and cab in Jamaica Street, on the 30th inst, and was fined 7s 6d, with the alternative of eight days' imprisonment – Charles McLauchlan and William Kelly, cabmen, were charged with quarrelling with each on, in Glassford St., on the 30th inst. McLauchlan failed to appear, and forfeited a pledge of 10s 6d. Kelly was found guilty on evidence and was fined 7s 6d. or eight days. On the same day Cecilia Underwood was charged with keeping a brothel at 68 Glassford Street. She too failed to appear on forfeited a pledge of £10.

Sensational cases, such as murder, were followed in breathless detail in local newspapers, as were the public execution of prisoners which, until 1865, took place in front of the Justiciary Building, facing Glasgow Green; after that date they were carried out inside Duke Street Prison until 1928 when they were transferred to Barlinnie Prison (last hanging in 1960). Capital sentences could be handed out for a surprising variety of cases. In June 1820, Richard Smith, a 16-year-old from Calton was executed for the crimes of housebreaking and theft, as reported in the *Glasgow Herald* on 2 June 1820:

> The unhappy youth ascended the scaffold with a firm step, bowed to the crowd, and after praying for a short time, in a kneeling posture, he flung the signal with him. Care had been taken to give him a sufficient fall, and he expired almost without a struggle. After hanging the allotted time, the corpse was taken down and delivered to his relatives.

While in prison, Smith had dictated a letter to his fellow prisoners urging them against keeping bad company 'and to avoid, in particular, that of loose women'.

Chapter 15

LOCAL DETAIL

Family history should be about more than just gathering names, dates and places. Tracing your ancestors should involve getting to know about the times and conditions in which they lived. Newspapers, maps and old photographs are a great way to add to the knowledge you have gleaned from certificates and census returns. Sometimes newspapers name our ancestors but at other times we will need to think a little more laterally, searching for stories about the places they lived and worked. Once you have found out where your forebears lived and are buried visit the places if you can – you may be lucky and some of the old houses and buildings mentioned in the records will have survived. Visiting such places can give you a better idea of the world your ancestors inhabited.

LOCAL PHOTOGRAPHS

The **Mitchell Library** holds tens of thousands of photographs from the early days of photography to present-day digital images including:

- Main photographic collection – a cumulative collection of over 10,000 photographs, which do not form any part of another archival group.
- Photographic survey of Glasgow schools, *c.* 1916 and *c.* 1960.
- Clyde Navigation Trust photographs – including groups and individual portraits, construction of works, buildings and sheds, cranes and equipment, ships and views of the Clyde (including aerial views).

- Parker Smiths of Jordanhill – includes a series of photographs, travel albums, family albums, glass negatives, portraiture, *cartes des visites*, daguerreotypes and ambrotypes dating from *c.* 1850–1920.

Many of its photographs are available on the Virtual Mitchell website, http://www.mitchelllibrary.org/virtualmitchell and the Glasgow Story website at http://www.theglasgowstory.com/.

Glasgow University has a magnificent photographic archive with material dating from the 1840s and including original calotype negatives and salted paper prints produced by the partnership of renowned Scottish photographers **D.O. Hill** and **Robert Adamson**. Its major collections of photographs are:

- Ashton – a collection of over 3,000 glass lantern slides featuring architecture and scenes of everyday life, 1890–1925.
- Bruce – over 1,200 stereoscopic glass photographic negatives made by William Speirs Bruce (1867–1921) on Arctic and Antarctic expeditions between 1899 and 1914.
- Dougan – includes work by photographic pioneers Hill and Adamson, early professionals Robert Macpherson and Samuel Bourne and interesting examples by amateurs. Over 200 bound volumes and albums, 1840s–early twentieth century.

Digitised photographic material is available online. For details visit the website at http://www.gla.ac.uk/services/specialcollections/searchbysubject/photography/.

MAPS, GAZETTEERS AND PLANS ARCHIVES

Maps and plans are invaluable source for local historians but it is important to remember when consulting them that boundaries change over the centuries. Boundary extensions in Glasgow during the second half of the nineteenth century and the first half of the twentieth century swallowed up parts of Lanarkshire, Renfrewshire

Local Detail

and Dunbartonshire, including over a dozen suburban burghs, of which the largest were Govan and Partick.

By the Local Government (Scotland) Act 1889 the city was placed entirely in the county of Lanark, the districts then transferred having previously belonged to the shires of Dunbarton and Renfrew. Therefore in older maps Glasgow will be found within the area of the pre-1975 county of Lanarkshire, from 1975 to 1996 it will appear within Strathclyde Region; current maps will generally show Glasgow as one of thirty-two Council Areas in Scotland.

The earliest map or plan of Glasgow appears in *Blaeu's Atlas* of 1694. It comes from a 1596 survey by Timothy Pont of the nether ward of Clydesdale, but the scale is too small to show any details of the city. In 1734 James Watt senior published a map entitled 'The River of Clyde' in which the city is shown in enough detail to indicate the major streets. The first plan to set out in detail most of the streets and important buildings was published in 1773 as an insert in Charles Ross's 'Map of the shire of Lanark'. It was drawn to a scale of 6in = 1 mile. John McArthur's 'Plan of the City of Glasgow, Gorbells, and Calton in four sheets' was published in 1778.

A part of Blaeu's 1654 map of Scotland. Modern Govan is at the site labelled 'Mekle Gouan' ('Big Govan').

By the beginning of the nineteenth century the demand for guide books led to the publication of two volumes with useful fold-out maps. The first of these was the *Picture of Glasgow*, first published by R. Chapman in 1806, and its companion *Glasgow Delineated*, first published in 1821.

Between 1858 and 1865, the Ordnance Survey published three separate map series which cover Glasgow – a town plan at 1:500 (on 155 sheets), a detailed County Series at 1:2500 (on 12 sheets) and the more general County Series at 1:10560. Fortunately, the whole of the city is covered on one sheet of the 1:10560 County Series of Lanarkshire (sheet VI). By the early 1850s the Ordnance Survey began to publish sheets covering Glasgow in scales of 6in and 25in to the mile. The second edition of the Glasgow sheets was published at the turn of the century when the city was at its height. In the 1890s the Ordnance Survey brought out a map of the city to the scale of 10½in to 1 mile which enables lamp posts, tenement closes and individual trees to be identified.

The **Mitchell Library** holds an extensive collection of maps and atlases with some 35,000 sheet maps and 300 atlases. These range from a 1647 edition of an early world atlas, *Theatrum Orbis Terrarum* by Joan Blaeu, to current editions of maps published by the Ordnance Survey.

There are several editions of Ordnance Survey maps at various scales produced for Lanarkshire and its surrounding areas throughout the nineteenth and twentieth centuries:

- 1860.
- 1896.
- 1913.
- c. 1934.
- Later dates in the twentieth century at different scales.

The Mitchell Library holds in its Special Collections Post Office maps of Glasgow during the nineteenth and twentieth centuries. In addition, it holds various administrative maps including those

Local Detail

showing the Poor Law districts, sasine divisions, Church of Scotland churches and schools within the city.

The **City Archives** also hold many feuing, rental and estate plans for certain areas within Glasgow and its surrounding environs. Feuing was the term used in Scots law to describe the process of selling a piece of land. Feuing and renting plans can show the boundaries of the property being sold or rented. These plans can be found in the records of the Town Clerk (Ref. D-TC13) and solicitors as well as in **Family and Estate Records**. Estate plans, which can give the names of tenants and show the location of their home, are often found in the collections of landed families, such as:

- Maxwells of Pollok (Ref. T-PM).
- Blythswood Estate (Ref. TD234).

Estate plans are also found in the records of solicitors. For example, Glasgow City Archives holds the papers of A.J. & A. Graham (Ref. T-AG), among others.

The collections of the City Archives also include maps and plans of areas that were previously part of Glasgow, such as Rutherglen (Ref. RU11). For more details see the website at https://www.glasgow life.org.uk/libraries/the-mitchell-library/special-collections/Documents/Early%20Glasgow%20Maps.pdf.

Glasgow University has an extentive map collection that shows the growth of the city from 1654 to the present day and is featured online at http://www.gla.ac.uk/services/library/collections/virtualdisplays/mapsofglasgowhistoricaltodigital/.

ScotlandsPlaces is a website that allows users to search across different national databases using geographic locations. The user is able to enter a place name or a coordinate to search across these collections or they can use the mapping in the website to both define and refine their search. ScotlandsPlaces website is http://www.scotlandsplaces.gov.uk/search/partner/glasgow.

The Saltmarket, photographed by Duncan Brown in the 1880s or 1890s. (Glasgow School of Art Archives)

Local Detail

Architectural Plans
If you are interested in learning more about the buildings in which your ancestors lived, you may like to search Glasgow City Archives' collection of architectural plans. The **Glasgow Archives** hold plans for Glasgow (1885–2006) as well as plans for the annexed burghs:

- Govan (1870–1912).
- Hillhead (1873–1891).
- Maryhill (1876).
- Partick (1873–1912).
- Pollokshaws (1893–1912).
- Pollokshields East (1880–7).

Its collections also include plans for Rutherglen (1872–1975). Additionally, the City Archives hold a selection of building plans for the parts of other counties that became part of Glasgow, principally Lanarkshire (1930–75) but also a small number for Dunbartonshire (1900–38) and Renfrewshire (1919–25).

You can access digitised copies of various maps on the NLS website at http://maps.nls.uk/.

NEWSPAPERS
Glasgow's first newspaper appeared on 14 November 1715. It was originally called the *Glasgow Courant, Containing the Occurrences Both at Home and Abroad*, appeared three times a week, on Tuesdays, Thursdays and Saturdays, and cost 3½d. The name was changed to the *West Country Intelligence* after only four issues, and only published sixty-seven issues. The *Glasgow Journal* was founded in 1741 as a weekly and ran until well into the next century. A second *Glasgow Courant*, another weekly, began publication on 21 October 1745 and soon gained a greater readership than the *Journal* thanks partly to its social news and advertisements. The *Glasgow Advertiser*, which first appeared on 27 January 1783, was a much more ambitious publication. In 1805 it adopted the name by which it is still known, the *Glasgow Herald*.

Genealogical information to be found in newspapers relates to fairly well-defined social groups. First, the doings of the nobility were covered in detail, particularly their births, deaths and marriages. Next, in terms of coverage, are the merchants and professional classes of the towns in which the newspapers were published. These would include barristers and solicitors, doctors, masters of schools, military officers and clergy as well as the more prosperous business people. After them would come the less well-off traders, traceable largely through advertisements. The local poor or working classes tend only to be picked up in reports of trials or the accounts of local boards of guardians, town commissioners and county councils. The drawback in using newspapers for genealogy is that you generally need to have a fairly precise date for an event before venturing to hunt for coverage, since indexes are limited.

Newspapers provided unique human interest stories about the city and its people, the sort of thing which will not appear in the major history books. The following story, for example, provides a unique insight into to the trials and tribulations to which Glasgow evacuees were subject to during the Second World War:

80 Miles on Fairy Cycle.
An eight-year-old evacuee to the Lochgair district of Argyll set out on his fairy cycle on an 80-mile journey to his home in Glasgow. He rode throughout the day and far into the night through some of Scotland's most desolate country.

He took 'in his stride' the famous Rest-and-be Thankful, and at three o'clock in the morning he reached his home and his mother, to see whom he had undertaken his adventurous journey. His first words when taken back to Lochgair were: 'I hope you haven't been worrying about me'. For this remarkable adventure, the boy chose a fairy cycle without a seat. At Arrochar he bought a bottle of lemonade and some biscuits. He covered the distance from Lochgair to Glasgow in 18 hours – at an average speed of 4½ miles per hour.

The lad did not tell any of his chums of his intention before

Local Detail

setting out, and, when he failed to return to his billet, search parties were organized.

The Mitchell Library has an extensive collection of local and national newspapers, most of them available on microfilm. Holdings are listed in the Periodicals Catalogue or can be searched online via the SALSER database. Only the *Glasgow Herald* has an index: 1906–84.

The resources include:

- *Glasgow Herald*.
- *Evening Times*.
- *Evening Citizen*.
- *Daily Record*.
- *Bulletin*.
- *Govan Press*.
- *The Times*.
- *Daily Telegraph*.
- *Scotsman*.
- *Guardian*.

Extended coverage of the *Glasgow Herald* is available online at Google covering the period 1806–1990. The collection is not complete, and appears to be a work in progress. Nevertheless, it is free, and can certainly be browsed as well as searched. Google also has the *Glasgow Advertiser* from 1789–1801 and the *Evening Times*, November 1900–July 1914, on the site at http://news.google.com/newspapers.

The **British Newspaper Archive** is a wonderful resource if you are searching for Scottish ancestors. For a monthly or yearly subscription you can assess a number of Glasgow newspapers including:

- *Glasgow Citizen*, 1844–5.
- *Glasgow Constitutional*, 1853–5.
- *Glasgow Courant*, 1745–58.
- *Glasgow Evening Citizen*, 1870.

- *Glasgow Free Press*, 1853–68.
- *Glasgow Gazette*, 1849–52.
- *Glasgow Herald*, 1820–1900.
- *Glasgow Morning Journal*, 1858–65.
- *Glasgow Saturday Post*, 1861–84.
- *Glasgow Sentinel*, 1850–65.

See http://www.britishnewspaperarchive.co.uk/.

If you live in Scotland you can access many Scottish newspapers through the NLS's 'Licensed digital collections' (free): all you have to do is register. The NLS also has a large collection of newspapers on microfilm that are free to view in person.

THE *STATISTICAL ACCOUNTS OF SCOTLAND*

The *Old (or First) Statistical Account of Scotland* was published between 1791 and 1799 by Sir John Sinclair of Ulbster. The *New (or Second) Statistical Account of Scotland* was published under the auspices of the General Assembly of the Church of Scotland between 1834 and 1845. The *Third Statistical Account of Scotland* was initiated after the Second World War and followed a similar parish format to the earlier accounts. The first volume, covering Ayrshire, was published in 1951. Ultimately, it was more rigorous and wide-ranging than either of its predecessors, covering industry, transport, culture and demographics.

The two earlier *Statistical Accounts of Scotland* are among the best contemporary reports of life during the agricultural and industrial revolutions in Europe. These volumes provide a variety of fascinating information in these sometimes idiosyncratic descriptions of our ancestors' parishes, which were compiled by the local ministers. Vol. 5 of the 1790s' *Statistical Account of Scotland* covers Elgyn, Montrose, Moulin, Logierait, Gordon, Pitsligo, Scoonie, Dumfries, Menmuir, Portmoak, Laurence-kirk, Unst, Urquhart and Logy Wester, Mains of Fintry, Old Kilpatrick, Cambuslang, Slains, Inveraray, Tarves, Currie, Fettercairn, Cathcart, Lochlee, Craigie, Strachan, Ceres, Symington, Holme, Keith, Cruden, North Berwick,

Local Detail

Ochiltree, Spott, Brechin, Inverchaolain, Dunbar, Glasgow, Gorbals, Port-Glasgow and Greenock. Vol. 19 of the 1830s' Account covers Lanark. You can assess them online at http://edina.ac.uk/statacc/ or http://www. electricscotland.com.

When the strong clerical input into the *Statistical Accounts* is considered it is not surprising that the volume for Scotland includes the following record of clerical pay and conditions:

> It has been said, that clergymen in the discharge of the sacred duties of their office belong to no particular class of society, mixing, as they necessarily do, with the high, the low, and the middle grades. In Glasgow the clergymen have always been highly respectable, and at no period more so than at present. The Established churches in Glasgow are all uncollegiate. The ministers prepare and preach two sermons every Sunday, and in rotation preach on Thursdays in St Mary's Church, and Hope Street and St Mary's Churches on Sunday evenings. They preach occasional charity and missionary sermons. They examine the youth of their congregations in class meetings, and give partial ministerial visitations in the families of their parishioners. To visit the whole in the present overgrown state of the parishes would be next to impossible. They visit the sick, and assist the kirk-session in the proper distribution of the poors' funds; – they superintend the schools in their parishes, – and, in obedience to the wishes of the pious founders of some of the benevolent institutions of the city, they share the management with the magistrates; and their attendance on funerals, kirk-sessions, presbyteries, synods, and general assemblies, occupies a considerable portion of their time. The bare recital of the above must convince every one of the laborious duties of a city parochial clergyman; and as to pecuniary remuneration, it is barely sufficient for present purposes, leaving little or no provision in case of a widowed family.

Appendix

SCOTTISH WEBSITES

Scotland is a world leader in providing family history information online. The best websites are the following:

Scotlands People
www.scotlandspeople.gov.uk
The most useful website is ScotlandsPeople, the official government source of genealogical data for Scotland with almost 90 million records to access. Researchers can download images for a fee from the fully indexed Scottish statutory records of births, deaths and marriages from 1855–2006, census records from 1841–1911 and indexes of the church baptisms, deaths and burials and marriages that took place from 1538–1854 and digitised wills and testaments from Scotland's National Archives and Scottish Catholic Archives records.

Scottish Archive Network (SCAN)
http://www.scan.org.uk/index.html
This is a great site if you are trying to trace the whereabouts of particular record collection because it provides a portal that allows you to search the electronic catalogues of more than fifty Scottish archives.

Scots Origins
http://www.scotsorigins.com/
A source of genealogical data for Scotland which includes an online Scots Origins Discussion Group.

Appendix

Scottish Genealogy Society
http://www.scotsgenealogy.com/
The aims of the society are to promote research into Scottish family history and to undertake the collection, exchange and publication of material relating to genealogy. The society, based in Edinburgh and run by volunteers, can advise you at all stages in your research.

National Library of Scotland
http://www.nls.uk
The biggest library in Scotland, the NLS has a wide range of genealogical information which should be of interest to family historians.

Public Libraries Online
http://dspace.dial.pipex.com/town/square/ac940/weblibs.html
A comprehensive portal listing all of the public libraries alphabetically.

ScotlandsPlaces
www.scotlandsplaces.gov.uk
ScotlandsPlaces is a partnership site created by the NRS, the Royal Commission for Ancient and Historical Records for Scotland and the Geographical Information Systems Department of the University of Edinburgh with assistance from the Scottish government. It is essentially a geographical companion site to ScotlandsPeople, and allows users to search for records concerning a location across various different national databases. The website includes free access to such collections as the 1797 Farm Horse Tax.

ScotlandGeneb Project
http://www.scotlandgenweb.org/news.php
Part of the British Isles GenWeb Project, this page serves as a local resource index page for Scottish genealogy research. It provides a link to county pages, provides look-up resources, transcribed data and an invaluable guide to family history societies across Scotland.

The Scottish Emigration Database
http://www.abdn.ac.uk/emigration/
The Scottish Emigration Database currently contains the records of over 21,000 passengers who embarked at Glasgow and Greenock for non-European ports between 1 January and 30 April 1923, and at other Scottish ports between 1890 and 1960.

Registers of Scotland
http://www.ros.gov.uk/
Registers of Scotland is responsible for compiling and maintaining registers relating to property in Scotland. Property records are major sources for house and local history and, as property was frequently passed from one generation to the next, also an important genealogical source. Modern property registers can be used to locate living relatives.

The Scottish Association of Family History Societies
http://www.safhs.org.uk/
The Scottish Association of Family History Societies promotes and encourages the study of Scottish family history, and provides a forum for the exchange of information among members. Membership includes all established family history societies in Scotland, as well as several national and regional bodies throughout the world.

The Federation of Family History Societies
http://www.ffhs.org.uk/
UK-wide federation of genealogy societies.

Ancestral Scotland
http://www.ancestralscotland.com
A site containing useful hints, features and ancestral and surname searches, which links into the Scotlandspeople database.

Appendix

Electric Scotland
http://www.electricscotland.com/
The Electric Scotland website is the largest and most comprehensive site on the history and culture of Scotland and the Scots at home and abroad. A great educational and research resource with thousands of books on all aspects of Scottish history and culture available online.

The Glasgow and West of Scotland Family History Society
http://www.gwsfhs.org.uk/
The society was founded in 1977 with the aim of promoting the study of family history, particularly for those whose family history has links with Glasgow and the west of Scotland.

BIBLIOGRAPHY

Butt, John and George Gordon (eds), *Strathclyde: Changing Horizons* (1985)
Chapman, R., *The Picture of Glasgow* (1906)
Chapman, R., *The Topographical Picture of Glasgow in its Ancient and Modern State (1820)*
Cleland, J., *Statistical and Population Tables Relative to the City of Glasgow* (1828)
Cleland, J., *Annals of Glasgow* (1816)
Cochrane, Hugh, *Glasgow: The first 800 Years* (1975)
Cowan, J., *From Glasgow's Treasure Chest* (1951)
Crawford, Robert, *On Glasgow and Edinburgh* (2013)
Cunnison, J. and J.B.S. Gilfillan, *The City of Glasgow, Third Statistical Account of Scotland* (1958)
Daiches, David, *Glasgow* (1982), scholarly history
Doak, A.M. and A.M. Young, *Glasgow at a Glance* (1983)
Fisher, Joe, *The Glasgow Encyclopaedia* (1994)
Gibb, Andrew, *Glasgow: The Making of a City* (1983)
Gomme, A.H. and D. Walker, *Architecture of Glasgow* (1987)
Horsey, M., *Tenements & Towers: Glasgow Working-Class Housing 1890–1990* (1990)
Hume, John, *Industrial Archaeology of Glasgow* (1974)
MacGeorge, Andrew, *Old Glasgow, the Place and the People* (1888)
McKean, Charles, *Central Glasgow: An Illustrated Architectural Guide* (1993)
Malcolm, Sandra. *Old Glasgow and The Clyde: From the Archives of T. and R. Annan* (2005)
Marwick, J.D., *Early Glasgow* (1911)
Massie, Allan, *Glasgow: Portraits of a City* (1989)
Maver, Irene, *Glasgow* (2000)
Muir, J.H., *Glasgow in 1901* (1901)
Oakley, Charles, *The Second City* (1975)
Patton, J., *Glasgow: its municipal organisation and administration* (1896)

Bibliography

Reid, J.M., *Glasgow* (1956)
Reid, R., *Glasgow, Past and Present* (1884)
Russell, J.B., *Old Glasgow* (1891)
Small, G.P., *Greater Glasgow: An Illustrated Architectural Guide* (2008)
Urquhart, Gordon R., *Along Great Western Road: An Illustrated History of Glasgow's West End* (2000)
Williamson, Elizabeth (ed.), *The Buildings of Scotland: Glasgow* (1999)
Worsdall, Frank, *The Victorian City: Selection of Glasgow's Architecture* (1988)
Worsdall, Frank, *The City That Disappeared: Glasgow's Demolished Architecture* (1981)
Worsdall, Frank, *The Tenement: A Way of Life* (1979)

Guidebooks and Descriptions
An Account of the Principal Pleasure Tours in Scotland (1819, 1821)
Black, Adam and Charles Black, *Black's Picturesque Tourist of Scotland* (first edn 1840)
Chambers, Robert, *The Picture of Scotland*, 2 vols (1827)
Cook, Thomas, *Handbook of a Trip to Scotland* (1846)
Denholm, James, *The History of the City of Glasgow, To which is Added a Sketch of a Tour to Loch Lomond and the Falls of Clyde* (1798)
A Description of the Most Remarkable Highways and whole known fairs and Mercats in Scotland (1711)
Duncan, James, *The Scotch Itinerary, Containing the Roads through Scotland, on a New Plan* (1805)
The Gazetteer of Scotland (1803)
Heron, Robert, *Scotland Delineated: or a geographical Description of every Shire in Scotland* (1799)
Heron, Robert, *Scotland Described: or a Topographical Description of all the Counties of Scotland* (1797)
The New Picture of Scotland, 2 vols (1807)
Sinclair, Sir John (ed.), *The Statistical Account of Scotland (1791–9); The Second (New) Statistical Account (1834–45); The Third Statistical Account (1951)*
The Traveller's Guide, or a Topographical Description of Scotland (Edinburgh, 1798).

INDEX

Aberdeen 24, 25
accent 8–9
Act of Union 27–8
adoption 41
Albion Motors 58
Alexander Park 11, 155
American War of Independence 29, 142
Anderston 10, 58
Anniesland 12
apprenticeships 79, 112, 125, 146
architectural plans 186
archives 14–17
Argyle 41
army records 145–9
asylums 127–8

bailies 48
Baillieston 14
bakers 89
Balornock 11
Baptists 70–1, 77
barbers 89
Barlinnie 175
Barony workhouse 124, 125
Belgian refugees 139
Bellahouston 11
births, deaths and marriages 38–40
Blackhill 11
Bloody Friday 35
bone collectors 170–1
bonnet makers 89
boundary changes 10–14
bowling 161
Bridewell 173
Broomielaw 26, 137
burgess rolls 51
burgesses 51
burgh 23, 48–9
Burgh Court 176
burgh records 50–1

burgh schools 108
business records 87–93
Bute 41

Caledonian Railway Association 104
Caledonian Railway Company 58, 95, 96, 102
Calton 10, 165
canal records 97–9
canals 95–7
Carlyle, Dr Alexander 29
Carmunnock 14
Carmyle 11
Carriage Tax rolls 55
Carron Iron Works 28
Cart Tax rolls 55
Castlemilk 13
Cathcart 12
Catholic Church 47, 65, 69
Catholic emancipation 69
Catholic parish registers 36, 47, 76
Celtic FC 65, 134, 161
census records 36–8
Central station 102
Charles II 141
chemical works 82
child labour 79, 85–6
chimney sweeps 90
cholera 31, 121
church attendance 68–9
Church records 72–7
Church of Scotland 65–9, 70, 72–5
cinema 159
City of Glasgow District Council 49
City Improvement Trust 122
civil registration 38–41
Clyde Navigation Trust 98
Clydesdale Amateur Rowing Club 156
Clydeside Blitz 150
Clydewater Committee 34

Index

coach travel 94–5
coal industry 84–7, 96
colliers 85–7
Comet, The 83
Commonwealth Games 3
Consolidated schedule of Assessed Taxes 54
coopers 89
cordiners 89
corporation 13, 49, 59
cotton industry 79–81
court records 178–80
Craigton 11
cricket 161–2
Crosshill 11
Crossmyloof 11
Cumbernauld 13

Dawsholm 12
death records 40
deeds 64
Defoe, Daniel 2, 78
Dennistown 11
directories 91–3
Dodd, Ken 159
drivers, hackney carriages 90
Drumchapel 13
Duke Street Prison 173–5
Dumbarton 141
Dunbartonshire 41, 62, 63
Dundee 24, 25
Dunoon 57, 157

East Kilbride 13
Easterhouse 13
Edinburgh 24, 25
Edinburgh & Glasgow Railway Company 97, 99, 100, 101
  archive 104
Edinburgh and Glasgow Union Canal 97
education 108–19
Education (Scotland) Act 1872 109
electoral records 52–3
Empire Theatre 159

Episcopalians 67, 70, 77
Erskine 13
European City of Culture 3
evacuees 150–2
Evening Times Roll of Honour 148

Female Servants Tax 56
Finnieston 58
First World War 144–5, 148–9
Fleshers 89
Flodden, Battle of (1513) 141
football 159–61
football archives 163
Forth and Clyde Canal Company 95–7
Fox, George 67, 72
Free Church of Scotland 69
freemen 51

Gallowgate 120, 122, 177
Gardiners 89
Gillespie, Robert 33, 157
Glasgow & Ayrshire Railway 99
Glasgow cathedral 1, 22–3, 65
Glasgow City Archives 41
Glasgow Corporation 13, 49, 59
Glasgow Corporation records 51, 52
Glasgow Corporation Tramways 106–7
Glasgow District Council 49
Glasgow Fair 156
Glasgow & Garnkirk Railway 99
Glasgow Golf Club 162
Glasgow Grammar School 109
Glasgow Green 155–6
Glasgow Green Prison 175
Glasgow & Greenock Railway 99, 157
Glasgow history 22–34
Glasgow Militia 146
Glasgow, Paisley and Ardrossan Canal 96–7
Glasgow School Board 110
Glasgow & South Western Railway Company 96–7, 102
  archives 104
Glasgow Town Council 49
Glasgow University 23

Glasgow University Rowing Club 156
Glasgow & West of Scotland Family
  History Society 8
Glasgow workhouse 124, 125
golf 162
Gorbals 10, 11, 13, 57, 65, 83, 85, 112,
  122, 135, 171
Gorbals workhouse 124
Govan 11, 12, 13, 53, 63, 84, 85, 89, 90,
  96, 106, 116, 124, 125, 127, 128, 131,
  171, 183, 187, 189
Govan workhouse 124, 125
Govanhill 10, 11
graveyards 18–29
Great Disruption 69
Greenock 29, 92, 94, 98, 127, 130, 151,
  157

health 120–2
Hearth Tax 55–6
High Court of Judiciary 177
Highland Light Infantry 143–5
Hillhead 10, 11, 187
Horse Tax rolls 55
hospital records 127
hospitals 125–27
House of Correction 173
House of Refuge 166
Hutchesontown 156

Ibrox 13
industrial schools 166
Inhabited House Tax 54
inheritance 43–4
inventories 44
Irish Famine 132, 135
Irish migration 130–4, 171
iron industry 28, 81–2
Italian migrants 135–7

Jacobite Risings 141–2
Jewish migrants 135
Jewish records 16, 140
Jocelin of Furness 22
Jocelin, Bishop of Glasgow 23, 50

Johnstone 96
Jordanhill 12
judicial system 176–80
juvenile crime 166, 173–4

Kelvingrove Art Gallery and Museum 3
Kelvingrove Park 11, 155
Kelvinside 11, 165
Kentigern 1, 22, 23
Kilbride 13–14
Kinning Park 11
Kirk sessions 65–6, 168–9

Lanark 13
Lanarkshire 62, 63
land and property ownership 57–9
landed estate records 59–61
Langside 11
Lauder, Sir Harry 158
Laurel, Stan 158, 159
Licences, Register of 90–1, 159
linen industry 79
local government 48–53
local history 7–8
London, Midland & Scottish Railway
  102
London & Northern Eastern Railway
  102

Mackintosh, Charles Rennie 3
Male Servant Tax rolls 56
Maltmen 89
maps 182–5
marriages 38–9
  irregular 46–7
  regular 46
Mary, Queen of Scots 141
Maryhill 10, 11, 13
Masons 89
Maxwell Estate 58
merchants 48–9, 88
Merchants House 88–9
  records of Merchants House 89
Methodists 71
Metropole Theatre 158

Index

migration
  Highland 69, 129–30
  Irish 69, 130–4
  Lowland 134–5
Militia records 146
Mitchell Library 2, 8, 14–15
moneylenders 90
Monkland Canal 96, 98
Monkland & Kirkintilloch Railway archives 98, 104
Monklands 28
Monumental Inscriptions 20
mortcloth 73
Mount Florida 11
Mount Vernon 13
Mungo 1, 22
Municipal Police Board 49, 169–70
muster rolls 146

National Register of Archives 61
navvies 101
Necropolis 19
Newark 26
Newlands 12
newspapers 187–90
Nonconformist records 77
North British Locomotive Collection 103
North British Railway 101, 102, 103

Old Parish Records 20, 45–7
Old Pollock 58
Orange Order 131

Paisley 96
parliamentary returns of 1872 and 1873 60–1
Partick 11, 12, 13, 84, 106, 137, 159, 187
Partick Thistle FC 161
passport records 139
Penny Mobs 168
People's Palace and Winter Gardens 156
Perth 24

pew renting 67–9
photographs 181–2
police 165–73
  records 172–3
Police Commissioners 49
Poll Tax 56
Pollokshaws 187
Pollokshields 10, 11, 58, 187
Polmadie 11
Poor Law 122–4
  records 122–5
population 12, 13, 25, 27
Port Dundas 95
Port Glasgow 26, 27, 29
Porters 90
Possilpark 11
Presbyterianism 65–9
prisons 173–6
  records 175–6
probate records 44–5
provost 48
public houses 153, 159
publicans 90

Quakers 67, 72
Queen's Park 11, 155
Queen's Park FC 161
Queen's Street station 99

railways 99–103
railway records 103–5
Rangers 65, 131, 161, 162
Reformation 24, 25
Register of Sasines 61–2
registration of births, deaths and marriages 38–40
Renfrewshire 41, 62, 63
River Clyde Police 172–3
rolls of honour 148–9
Roman Catholic Church 67, 76
rowing 156
Royal College of Physicians & Surgeons of Glasgow 16
Royal Conservatoire of Scotland Archives & Collections 163

Russell, Dr J.B. 31
Rutherglen 13, 63

St Enoch's station 102
Saltmarket 32, 120, 122, 156, 165, 173, 177
sasines 61–2
school attendance 108–9
school records
  Allan Glen School 112
  City School 110
  Glasgow Academy 112
  Glasgow Burgh or Grammar School 111
  Glasgow High School 113
  Hutcheson Grammar School 112
  John Street School 110
  Kelvinside Academy 112
  Kent Road School 110
  Laurel Bank School 114
  Park School 114
  St Aloysius College 110
  St Mungo's Academy 110
  Westborne School 114
  Whitehill School 110
  Woodside School 110
ScotlandsPeople 36
ScotlandsPlaces 185, 193
Scotstoun 12, 58
Scottish Catholic Archives 47, 76
Scottish Jewish Archives 16, 140
Scottish Theatre Archive 162
Second World War 145, 150–2
Shawlands 11
Sheriff's Court 177
Shettleston 12
shipbuilding 82–4
Skinners 89
smallpox 121
Smollett, Tobias 31
Springboig 13
Springburn 11, 103
Statistical Accounts 79, 190–1
Stirling 151
Stranthbungo 11

Strathclyde Regional Council 13, 49
Street Traders 90
Stuart, Prince Charles Edward 142
Surgeons 16, 89
surnames 3–7

tailors 89
taxation records 53–6
teachers 115–16
Teneu 22
Theatre Royal 158
tobacco 28
'Tobacco Lords' 28, 29, 78–9
Tolbooth 173, 177
Tollcross 12, 28, 85
Tontine Coffee House 153–5
town council 48–9, 67
Trades House, records of 89
trams 105–6
transport 94–107
Trongate 122, 165, 170
tuberculosis 121
Tucker, Thomas 26
typhus 121

underground railway 102, 105–6
universities 114–15
  Caledonian 114
  Glasgow 114, 116–18
  Strathcylde 114–15

valuation records 63–4
voters' rolls 52–3

weavers 89
websites 192–5
West of Scotland Cricket Club 159, 162
wills and testamentary records 41–4
Window Cleaners 90
Window Tax 54–5
Wordsworth, Dorothy 30
workhouse 122–5
Wrights 89